straw sculpture

STRAW SCULPTURE

techniques and projects

by Ruth S. Hibbs

DRAKE PUBLISHERS INC.   NEW YORK

Published in 1974 by
Drake Publishers Inc.
381 Park Avenue South
New York, New York 10016

Library of Congress Cataloging in Publication Data
Hibbs, Ruth.
  Straw sculpture: techniques and projects
  1. Straw work.   I. Title.
TT876.H5   746.4'1   74-6117
ISBN 0-87749-676-5

Printed in the United States of America

table of contents

acknowledgments

For some years I have noted with interest straw forms created as folk craft in Europe, Asia, North America, South America, and elsewhere and have been impressed with the universality of this use of grain straw as a craft medium. I wish to acknowledge all those who have contributed to the structuring of plant and animal forms in straw.

I am especially grateful to Bess Ferguson for helpful suggestions concerning the presentation of instructional materials and to Kathryn Seibel, in whose workshop I was introduced to straw craft. Also, Mary Metcalf and Marie Hibbs, both active straw crafters, have generously shared their techniques. I have appreciated seeing straw objects from many different countries in the art collections of Marie Budolfson, Frances Smith, Lorraine French, Lois Carr, Sue Oliver, Lavinia Strickland, Marguerite Bensend, and Baerbel Russell; and Leila Compton has kindly shared her knowledge of folklore associated with straw art in England.

introduction

For those of us who have been privileged as children to spend long unprogrammed hours close to nature at harvest time, it is easy to identify in spirit with the peasant farmer and his wife who handled the grasses as they cut them with the sickle, and saw in them, not only their daily bread, but a potential medium of expression for their creative spirits. It was only natural that, as the approach of festival days sparked the urge to make gifts for family and friends and to decorate the house, the homemaker should reach for materials at hand, then twist and tie until her vision was realized.

As I worked with this folk craft, I became increasingly aware of its potential and now regard it as a valid art medium for those who will consistently apply the principles of good design. I find that it offers me a unique opportunity for creativity, and it is my hope that the basic techniques presented in this book, together with numerous applications, will provide the tools and stimuli to launch you on your own creative venture with straw.

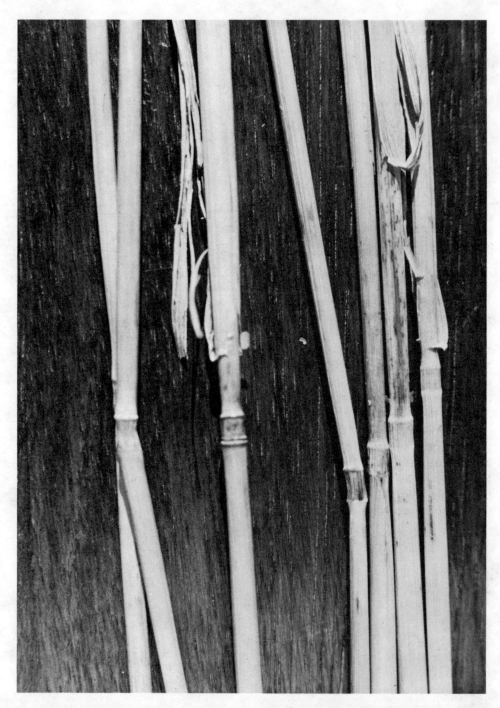

NODES, INTERNODES, AND HUSKS OF RYE STRAW.

Swing the shining sickle
Cut the ripened grain
Flash it in the sunlight
Swing it once again

Tie the golden grain heads
Into shining sheaves
Beautiful their colors
As the autumn leaves

—From an old song

materials

In straw sculpture, the designer's medium is rye straw. Because sections between the nodes of rye straw are quite long and because it is relatively tough, rye is preferable to wheat, oat, or barley straw for general use, although the others are quite satisfactory for many figures.

An excellent source of rye straw is the roadside adjacent to newly constructed highways. Rye is planted there as a nurse crop for new grass seedings. If you have a plot of land, you may want to plant your own patch of rye in the fall of the year and have it ready to harvest in the early summer. Farmers in most areas of the country will have a field of rye, but be sure to get your supply ahead of the harvester. The modern combines and balers do not handle the straw as gently as did the farmer with his hand-sickle. If you are not near an agricultural area, see the section in this book entitled Suppliers for a source of straw.

preparation of the straw

Gather the straw in early summer when it is golden ripe and before rain causes it to discolor or mildew.

Cut the standing plants close to the ground, taking care not to crush or bend the stems.

Spread the cut bundles in the sun or store them in an attic to dry.

Cut off all the heads and cut out all the nodes. (By aligning heads and also nodes, you can cut them from several straws at once.) When the straw is thoroughly dry, slip off all the husks.

Sort the husked straws into separate bundles of thick, medium, and thin
straws. Stand these sorted bundles on end in separate wide-mouthed
jars and store them for future use.

Before you begin the construction of a figure, submerge selected straws in a
pan or tub of water and allow them to soak overnight. Prolonged
soaking yellows the straws. So wet only as many as you plan to use
in a day. If you are in a hurry, pour boiling water over the straws
and soak them for an hour.

characteristics of rye straw

Each stalk has a grain head and three or more nodes. The grain heads on short
lengths of stalk make pleasing additions to arrangements of dried
plants or are beautiful when grouped alone. Grain heads may also
be used for manes and tails on straw horse figures or as woolly coats
for sheep.

A thin husk attached at each node covers the straw and terminates in a long,
grasslike leaf before it reaches the next node on the stalk. These
husks are beautifully glossy inside and can be used in split-straw
designs and in looped or coiled ornaments.

The husks and straws both have microscopic striations, or ridges and grooves,
that reflect light and give the straws and husks a metallic luster.
These tiny striae run up and down the straws but never crosswise.
Attention to the direction of these striations is important in working
out dark and light patterns in split-straw designs.

Sections of straw between nodes are thin at the top of a plant and become
increasingly thicker as they approach the base. The base sections
reach a maximum thickness of approximately ¼ inch, while some
top straws are extremely thin.

The lengths of internode sections at the top and midregion of a stalk may be
25 inches or more, but sections near the base are shorter.

Sections between nodes are slightly tapered. This feature makes it possible
to lengthen straws by telescoping the narrow end of one straw into
the wider end of another. As straws are being grouped for the construction of a figure, put all wide ends of straws at one extremity
of the bundle and all narrow ends at the other.

All straws are hollow. They can be split vertically and flattened, some to a
width of ¾ inch. Notice that the inside of the straw is less golden in
color and is lighter in value than the outside but that, like the outside, it also has striations.

The straws are brittle and will crack or split unless they are soaked in water before tying, bending, or flattening.

Interesting subtle variations of color appear occasionally in the straws, although the golden color is predominant. One of the most pleasing variations is a lovely violet shade that sometimes occurs.

working materials and tools

This list of suggested materials and tools is intended to help you in assembling the equipment you will need to begin your straw projects. You may wish to add to or subtract from this list as your experience with straw grows. Keep this equipment in a transparent plastic shoe box so that you can quickly put your hand on any tool or material you need.

FOR GENERAL USE

Seven-inch straight, sharp **scissors** for cutting straw and cord.

Nippers for cutting small wires.

Number 10 ecru **crochet cotton** for tying straws.

Number 4 **milliner's needle** (thin and about 2¼ inches long) for holding straws.

Number 8 **rubber bands** for holding straws.

Number 21 **florist's wire** (18-inch straight wire) for wiring parts that will remain bent.

Spools of fine **bead wire** (gold colored) for tying very small straw figures and for attaching some figures to backgrounds.

FOR SPLIT-STRAW WORK

X-Acto knife (or razor blade) and paper punch for cutting shapes from flattened straw.

Tweezers for manipulating small segments of split straw.

Masking tape for backing and extending widths of split straw.

White glue [such as Elmer's Glue-ALL® (Borden, Inc.)] that dries transparent. This will be used for gluing straw designs to fabric or wood mounts.

Five-eighths-inch gold sunburst **spangles** to use as accents with split-straw compositions.

Eye screws for hanging small plaques.

FOR THE CHILD AND ANGEL FIGURES

Small black, flat-headed **tacks** for eyes on some child figures.
Red flannel **fabric** for caps on some child figures.
Number 10 **crochet cotton** (red) for decorative accents.
Gold **cord** (about number 10 size) for weaving into wings, skirts, and sunbursts.
Wooden **beads,** 8mm and 10mm, for heads of angel and child figures.
Milkweed pods for mounting small figures.
A length of gold **sequins** to edge the pod.

FOR STRAW JEWELRY

Earring blanks.
Drop-style **earclips.**
Bell caps to use with the drop-style earclips.
Pin backs for brooches.
One-half-inch wooden **beads** to use with split-straw earrings.

FOR THE HAT

Curved **upholstery needle** for use in joining the strips of braid that make the hat. (A straight needle will not dig into a flat surface and come out easily, as is required in this operation.)
One-inch beige grosgrain **ribbon** for a sweatband.

FOR ANIMAL AND BIRD FIGURES

Quarter-inch red velvet **ribbon** for decorating the goat figure.
Three-fourths-inch gold-colored **sequins** to circle the eyes of the French hens.
One-half- and ⅝-inch wooden **beads** for the head and body of the bird.
Black **map tacks** for eyes.
Two-ply red **yarn** for decorative accents.

FOR SPIRAL TREES

Quarter-inch wooden **dowels** for the tree trunks.
Five-inch wooden **plaques** for the tree bases.

FOR DECORATIVE GIFT PAPERS

Blueprint paper.

FOR THE STYROFOAM PYRAMID

Wide **rubber bands** to fit the size pyramid you will be using.

FOR THE COLLAPSIBLE WALL-PANEL

Five-gauge clear **acetate.**

SUPPLIERS

In some areas of the country, certain essential items are difficult to find. I have therefore prepared this directory of suppliers to make it easier for you to locate needed supplies.

Art Supply Stores
  Clear acetate

Book and Stationery Stores
  Map tacks
  Rubber bands

Building Supply Stores
  Wooden dowels
  Wooden plaques

Craftsman Supply House
35 Browns Avenue
Scottsville, New York 14546
  Natural wood beads
  Sunburst spangles (gold)
  Beadcraft wire (gold)
  Drop-style earclips (gold)
  Bell caps (gold)
  Earring blanks (gold)
  Pin backs

Des Moines Blueprint Company
816 Locust
Des Moines, Iowa 50309
  Blueprint paper, available in 24-, 30-, 36-, and 42-inch widths in rolls 100 and 300 yards long. (The company will supply any cut sizes that you request.)

Fabric Stores
  Number 4 milliner's needles
  Curved upholstery needles
  Number 10 crochet cotton, ecru and red
  Colored yarn, lightweight
  Gold cord
  Quarter-inch red velvet ribbon
  Red flannel fabric

Florist Shops
  Number 21 florist's wire

Maid of Scandinavia Company
3245 Raleigh Avenue
Minneapolis, Minnesota 55416
    Five-inch wooden plaques

Paul Straight
Craft Supplies
Yarrow, Missouri 63501
    Rye straw
    Milkweed pods

Supreme Handicrafts
P.O. Box 395
Sioux Falls, South Dakota 57101
    Eye screws
    Gold bead wire
    Sunburst sequins (gold)
    Bell caps
    Drop-style earclips
    Earring blanks
    Pin backs

basic techniques

The mastery of a few basic techniques will make it possible for you to produce designs that are real works of art. Frequent reference will be made to these techniques in the section of the book entitled Applications.

BENDING

1 Use soaked straws.
2 Bend only one straw at a time.
3 Make the bend very sharp with the aid of your thumbnail.

TYING TWO-DIMENSIONAL FIGURES

1 Select wet straws of nearly equal thicknesses.
2 Cut them into 3-inch lengths.
3 Lay 10 of these lengths side by side on a flat surface.
4 Push a long, slender needle through their centers.
5 Wrap a length of number 10 crochet cotton (or cord of similar strength) around the 10 straws close to the needle. Make the cord go across the top and cross once underneath the straws.
6 Hold the straws flat with a finger of one hand while you pull one end of the cord firmly and steadily with the other, making the straws fan out.
7 Reverse hands and pull the other end of the cord until it is taut.
8 Tie a firm double knot close to the bundle of straw. Snip off the surplus cord and remove the needle.

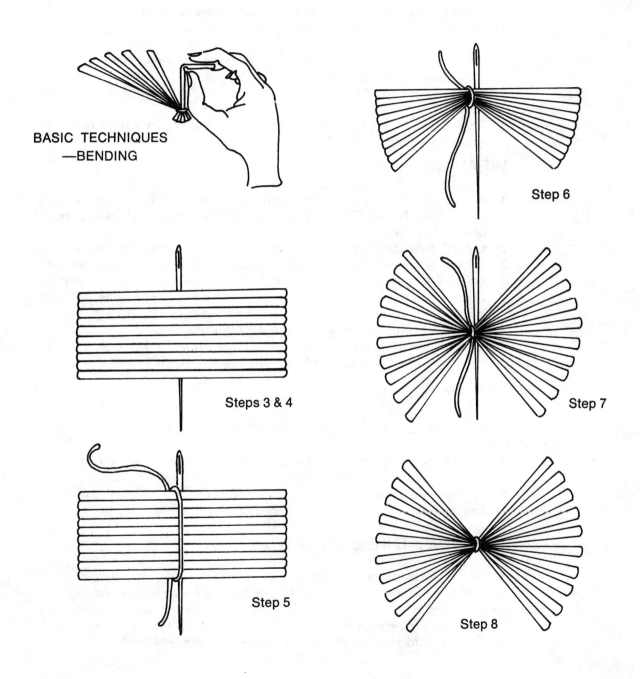

BASIC TECHNIQUES
—BENDING

Step 6

Steps 3 & 4

Step 7

Step 5

Step 8

TYING 2-DIMENSIONAL FIGURES

TYING THREE-DIMENSIONAL FIGURES

1 Select the required number of wet straws of nearly equal thicknesses.
2 Slip a small rubber band around the bundle to hold during the tying process.
3 Wrap a length of cord around the bundle twice, crossing once underneath and ending crossed on top.
4 Pull firmly and steadily on the ends of the cords until the bundle is completely compressed under the cord.
5 Tie a firm double knot close to the bundle. Snip off the excess cord and remove the rubber band.

WEAVING

1 In one hand hold a wet straw sunburst, made by following instructions under Tying Two-Dimensional Figures. With the other hand, loop a length of cord under one straw.
2 Cross the strands of cord once; then put them around the next straw.
3 Do the same with each succeeding straw. (Hold the forefinger between the two strands as you twist them and fit them over straws.) Cross the strands only once between straws and cross them in the same direction each time to maintain a uniform line of weaving.
4 Tie a firm double knot and snip off the excess cord.
5 With thumbs and fingertips, press the straws flat in the center of the sunburst and pull the woven cord outward into a neat, tight circle.

TELESCOPING

Notice that all straws taper slightly from one end to the other.

1 To lengthen, push the narrow end of one straw into the wide end of another, or push a thin straw into the open end of a thicker straw.
2 To telescope straws of the same thickness, cut a long diagonal slash from one end of a straw and slip it into the hollow end of another straw.

BRAIDING THREE STRAWS

1 Select 3 soaked straws of equal thicknesses.
2 Flatten the straws and tie them together with cord near one end.
3 Beginning with the middle straw lying on top of the 3, braid alternately with first the right straw then the left until the desired length is reached.
4 Tie with cord and snip off the excess ends of straw and cord.

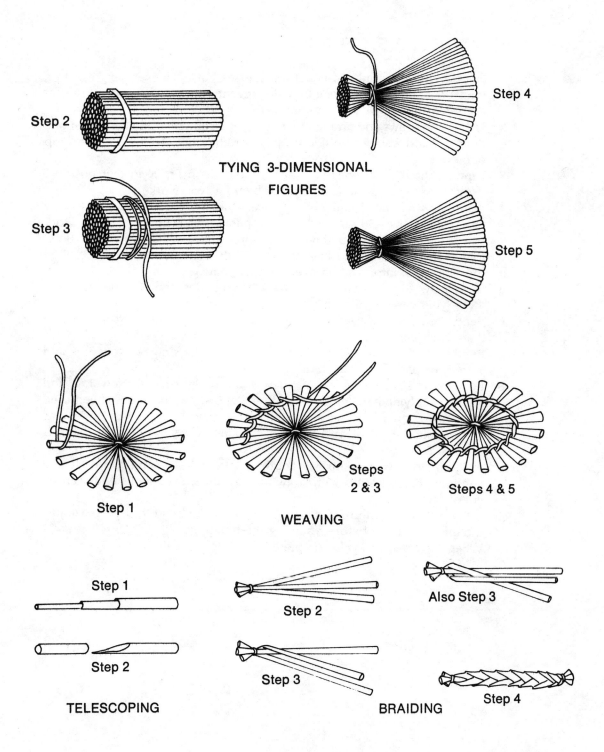

Step 2

Step 3

Step 4

TYING 3-DIMENSIONAL
FIGURES

Step 5

Step 1

Steps
2 & 3

Steps 4 & 5

WEAVING

Step 1

Step 2

Step 2

Step 3

Also Step 3

Step 4

TELESCOPING

BRAIDING

BRAIDING FIVE STRAWS

1 Select 5 soaked straws of equal thicknesses but of uneven lengths. (In a long braid the uneven lengths will prevent splicings from occurring at the same spot to weaken the braid.)

2 Flatten the straws and arrange them so that 3 straws lie side by side in one direction and 2 straws lie side by side at right angles to the 3 and on top of them.

3 Tape or stitch the 5 ends together to hold them firmly in that position. (Hold the straws flat on a tabletop or board as you work.)

4 Bend straw number 1 and weave it over straw number 2 and under straw number 3. Now 4, 5, and 1 are lying parallel to each other. (The work will progress more smoothly if the third straw is lifted up each time, folded sharply back, and held there until the first straw is in place, then dropped back into position over the first straw.)

5 Bend straw 4 and weave it over straw 5 and under straw 1. Now 2, 3, and 4 are lying parallel to each other.

6 Bend straw 2 and weave it over straw 3 and under straw 4. Now 5, 1, and 2 are lying parallel to each other.

7 Bend straw 5 and weave it over straw 1 and under straw 2. Now 3, 4, and 5 are lying parallel to each other.

8 Bend straw 3 and weave it over straw 4 and under straw 5. Now 1, 2, and 3 are again lying parallel to each other. All 5 straws have now been used for weaving one time and you are back to straw 1.

9 To continue, repeat steps 4 through 8 again and again until your braid is the desired length.

10 As each straw is used up, lay another flattened straw on top of it and continue. (Be generous with straw at the splice; extraneous ends can be cut off later.)

11 If the braiding is interrupted long enough for the braid to dry, resoak just the unfinished end before resuming the braiding.

12 When the braid is finally completed, tape or stitch the ends.

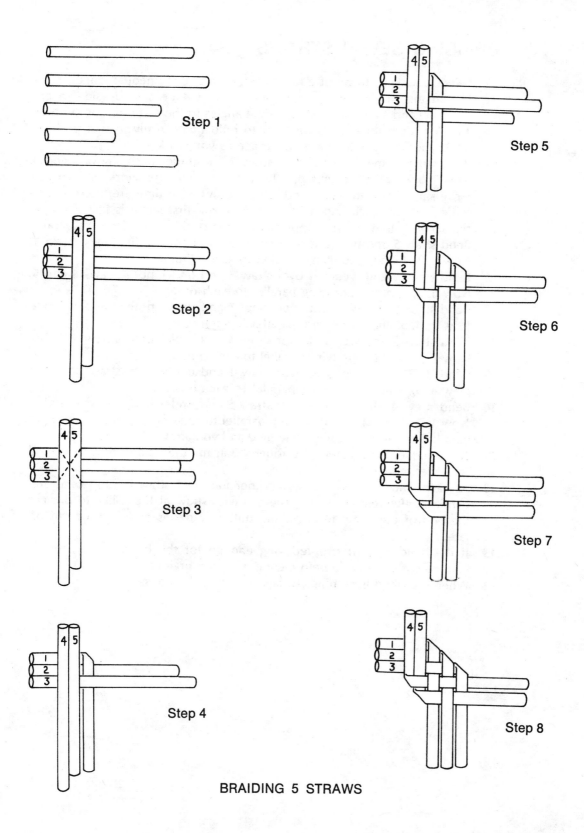

Step 1

Step 2

Step 3

Step 4

Step 5

Step 6

Step 7

Step 8

BRAIDING 5 STRAWS

BRAIDING SEVEN STRAWS

1 Select 7 soaked straws of equal thicknesses but of unequal lengths.

2 Flatten the straws and arrange them so that 4 lie side by side in one direction and 3 lie side by side at right angles to the 4 and on top of them.

3 Tape or stitch the 7 ends together to hold them firmly in that position. (Hold the straws flat on a hard surface as you work.)

4 Bend straw 1 and weave it over straw 2 and under both straws 3 and 4. Now 5, 6, 7, and 1 are lying parallel to each other. (The work will progress more smoothly if the third and fourth straws each time are lifted up and folded sharply back and held there until the first straw is in place over the second straw, then dropped back into position over the first straw.)

5 Bend straw 5 and weave it over straw 6 and under both straws 7 and 1. Now 2, 3, 4, and 5 are lying parallel to each other.

6 Bend straw 2 and weave it over straw 3 and under both straws 4 and 5. Now 6, 7, 1, and 2 are lying parallel to each other.

7 Bend straw 6 and weave it over straw 7 and under both straws 1 and 2. Now 3, 4, 5, and 6 are lying parallel to each other.

8 Bend straw 3 and weave it over straw 4 and under both straws 5 and 6. Now 7, 1, 2, and 3 are lying parallel to each other.

9 Bend straw 7 and weave it over straw 1 and under both straws 2 and 3. Now 4, 5, 6, and 7 are lying parallel to each other.

10 Bend straw 4 and weave it over straw 5 and under both straws 6 and 7. Now 1, 2, 3, and 4 are again lying parallel to each other. All 7 straws have now been used for weaving one time and you are back to straw 1.

11 To continue, repeat steps 4 through 10 again and again until your braid is the desired length.

12 As each straw is used up, lay another flattened straw on top of it and continue. (Remember to be generous with straw at the splice to prevent the end of the straw from pulling out; extraneous ends can be cut off later.)

13 If the braiding is interrupted long enough for the braid to dry, resoak just the unfinished end before continuing the braiding.

14 When the braid is completed, tape or stitch the ends.

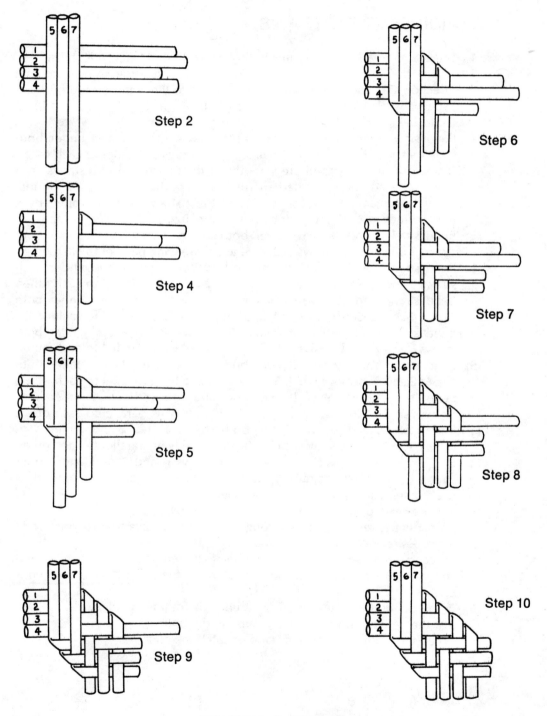

Step 2

Step 4

Step 5

Step 6

Step 7

Step 8

Step 9

Step 10

BRAIDING 7 STRAWS

BRAIDING NINE STRAWS

1   Select 9 soaked straws of uniform thicknesses but of uneven lengths.
2   Flatten the straws and arrange them so that 5 lie side by side in one direction and 4 lie side by side at right angles to the 5 and on top of them.
3   Tape or stitch the 9 ends together to hold them firmly in that position. (Hold the straws flat on a hard surface as you work.)
4   Bend straw 1 and weave it over both straws 2 and 3 and under both straws 4 and 5. Now straws 6, 7, 8, 9, and 1 are lying parallel to each other. (The work will progress more smoothly if the fourth and fifth straws each time are lifted up and folded sharply back and held there until the first straw is in place over the second and third straws, then dropped back into position over the first straw before moving on to the next step.)
5   Bend straw 6 and weave it over both straws 7 and 8 and under both straws 9 and 1. Now straws 2, 3, 4, 5, and 6 are lying parallel to each other.
6   Bend straw 2 and weave it over both straws 3 and 4 and under both straws 5 and 6. Now straws 7, 8, 9, 1, and 2 are lying parallel to each other.
7   Bend straw 7 and weave it over both straws 8 and 9 and under both straws 1 and 2. Now straws 3, 4, 5, 6, and 7 are lying parallel to each other.
8   Bend straw 3 and weave it over both straws 4 and 5 and under both straws 6 and 7. Now straws 8, 9, 1, 2, and 3 are lying parallel to each other.
9   Bend straw 8 and weave it over both straws 9 and 1 and under both straws 2 and 3. Now straws 4, 5, 6, 7, and 8 are lying parallel to each other.
10   Bend straw 4 and weave it over both straws 5 and 6 and under both straws 7 and 8. Now straws 9, 1, 2, 3, and 4 are lying parallel to each other.
11   Bend straw 9 and weave it over both straws 1 and 2 and under both straws 3 and 4. Now straws 5, 6, 7, 8, and 9 are lying parallel to each other.
12   Bend straw 5 and weave it over both straws 6 and 7 and under both straws 8 and 9. Now straws 1, 2, 3, 4, and 5 are again lying parallel to each other. All 9 straws have now been used for weaving one time and you are back to straw 1.
13   To continue, repeat steps 4 through 12 again and again until your braid is the desired length.
14   As each straw is used up, lay another flattened straw on top of it and continue. (Remember to allow extra straw at the splice; extraneous ends can be cut off later.)
15   If the braiding is interrupted long enough for the braid to dry, resoak just the unfinished end before resuming the braiding.
16   When the braid is completed, tape or stitch the ends.

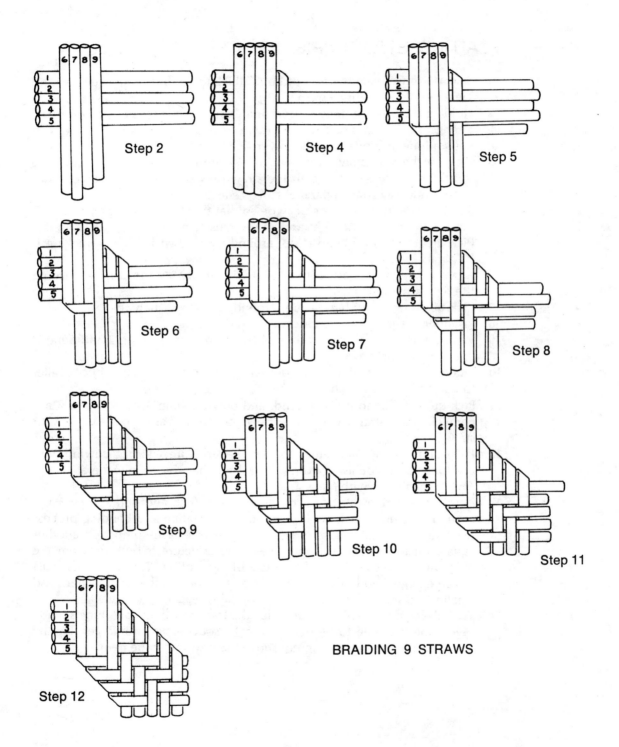

Step 2

Step 4

Step 5

Step 6

Step 7

Step 8

Step 9

Step 10

Step 11

BRAIDING 9 STRAWS

Step 12

PLAITING STRAW SPIRALS

1   Select 5 long soaked straws of equal thicknesses but of uneven lengths. Tie them togther ½ inch from the tip.

2   Holding this ½-inch nib between thumb and forefinger of your left hand, arrange the 5 straws so that 4 of them form a large plus sign in front of you and the fifth one is in the lower right quadrant.

3   Pick up the fifth straw and bend it up, around, and down behind the fourth straw. Be sure to crush the straw only where it loops around another straw. Lay straw 5 parallel to 1.

4   Rotate 90 degrees counterclockwise so that the 2 parallel straws (5 and 1) have now become the right arm of the plus sign.

5   Pick up straw 1 and bend it up, around, and down behind 5, making it lie parallel to 2.

6   Again rotate 90 degrees counterclockwise so that 1 and 2 have become the right arm of the plus sign.

7   Pick up straw 2 and bend it up, around, and down behind 1.

8   Rotate 90 degrees counterclockwise again.

9   With 2 and 3 parallel and in the right-arm position, pick up 3 and bend it up, around, and down behind 2.

10 Once more, rotate 90 degrees counterclockwise so that 3 and 4 lie parallel to each other at the right arm of the plus sign.

11 Pick up 4 and bend it up, around, and down behind 3. Now 4 and 5 are parallel. All 5 straws have now been bent once and you are back to straw 5.

12 If you hold 4 and 5 together so that the structure will not unwind, you can look at the side away from you and see that you have made a square. The ½-inch nib is within the square.

13 Turn the square away from you as it was at first, and bend straw 5 up, around, and down behind 4. Continue this rotating and bending process until you are back to 5, at which time you will have completed another square on top of the first one. The entire structure is built up from the resulting squares as they pile on top of each other. These squares must become larger and larger as the wide part of the spiral is approached, and smaller and smaller as the end of the spiral is reached.

14 To make squares become smaller, lay the last straw bent each time slightly below the next one to be bent. To make squares become larger, lay the last straw bent each time slightly above the next one to be bent.

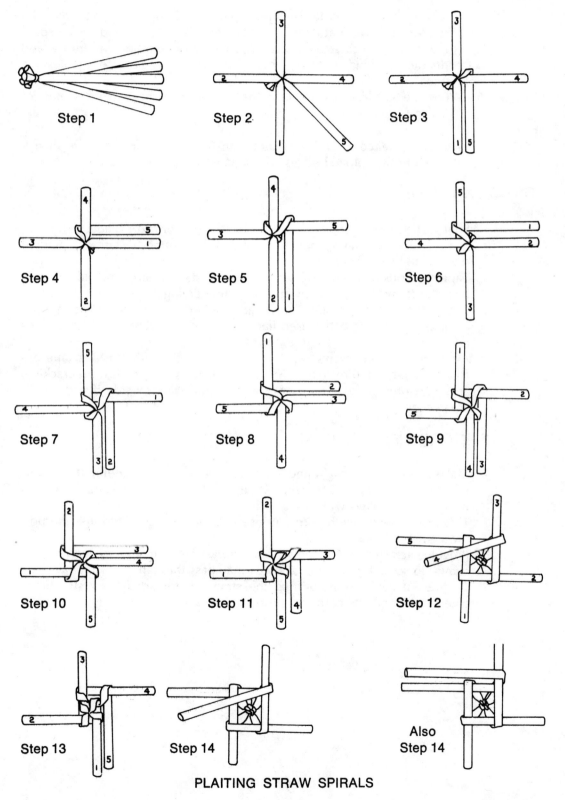

Step 1   Step 2   Step 3

Step 4   Step 5   Step 6

Step 7   Step 8   Step 9

Step 10   Step 11   Step 12

Step 13   Step 14   Also Step 14

PLAITING STRAW SPIRALS

15 After you have plaited to the widest part of the spiral, you may turn the piece over and work at decreasing the squares until the end of the spiral is reached. As each straw is used up, telescope another one into it and continue. Spiraling of the corners occurs naturally as the squares are formed.

16 When the smallest square closes the opening, tie the remaining ends of straw and clip them off.

The same plaited straw spiral form can be achieved using more than 5 straws, but the spiraled edges will be closer together.

SPLITTING

1 Split soaked straws lengthwise with a sharp knife or razor blade.
2 Flatten the split straws open and wrap them around a glass container if they are to be used curved.
3 Tape the ends of the straws together or tie narrow strips of old sheeting over the straws to hold them in place while drying.
4 Flatten the split straws open and weight them down overnight with a book or board if they are to be used flat. Press the wet straws flat with a moderately hot iron if you are in a hurry.
5 After the flattened straws are dry, cover the backs with masking tape before cutting them into shapes. This tape will keep the straws from cracking. Several widths of straw may be taped together side by side if wide strips are needed.

THREADING

1 Make a long, thin, straight needle from florist's wire by bending the end to form a narrow eye. (Too wide an eye will split the straw as it passes through. A crooked wire will do the same thing.)
2 Thread this needle with cord and use it to pull the cord through the hollow centers of straws.
3 Provide each straw with its own cord or pass a single cord through several straws. In some figures several cords may pass through a single straw.
4 To prevent cords from splitting the straws in threaded-straw structures, take short lengths of cord and tie at all intersections.

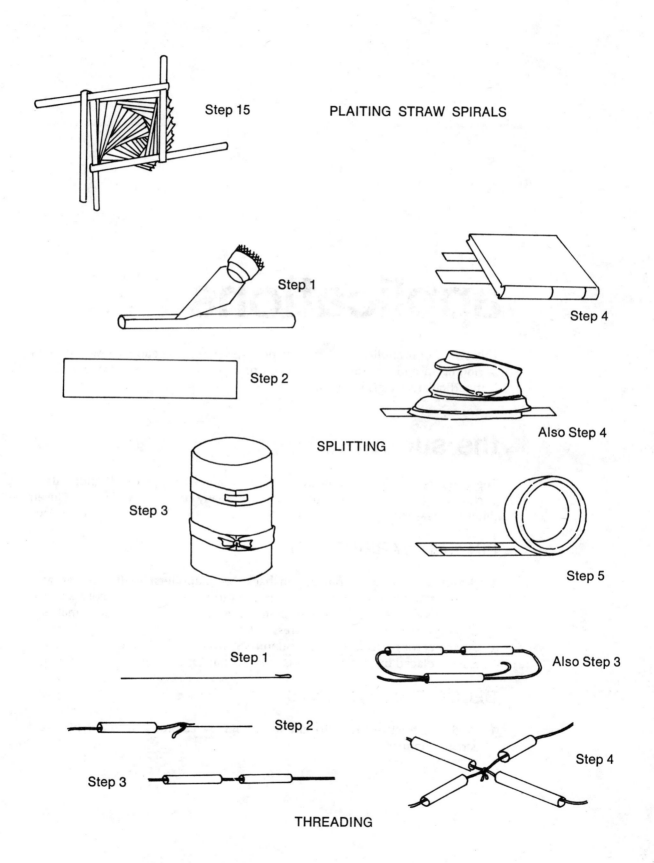

Step 15

PLAITING STRAW SPIRALS

Step 1

Step 4

Step 2

SPLITTING

Also Step 4

Step 3

Step 5

Step 1

Also Step 3

Step 2

Step 3

Step 4

THREADING

applications

This section on applications has not been prepared to read as a whole from beginning to end. Instructions for each project can be noted as a unit when that particular piece is being made.

the sunburst

The sunburst motif, the construction of which was explained under Basic Techniques (Tying and Weaving), may have many uses and variations. Eleven different ideas for its use are discussed in this section. You will think of others.

PIN AND EARRING SET

1 Attach a small safety pin or pin back (see Suppliers) to the center of a large straw sunburst. Weave gold cord in to replace the ecru cord and cut the ends of the rays of the sunburst to long, sharp points. This makes a striking ornament for a dark dress or hat.
2 Attach earring blanks to small sunbursts, which also should have the ecru cord replaced by gold cord. This makes a pair of earrings to match the pin.

DECORATIVE ACCENTS

1 Add a distinctive touch to gift wrappings by careful placement of a few straw sunbursts.

2 Provide just the right accents for a wall hanging or piece of creative stitchery by adding sunbursts in a variety of sizes.

3 Work tiny straw sunbursts into compositions with miniature dried plants and small sections of grain heads.

SUNBURST PIN AND EARRING SET

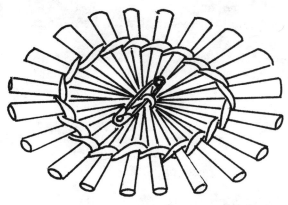

Step 1

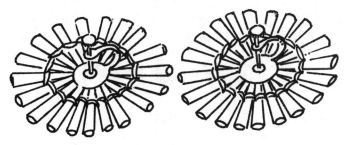

Step 2

WALL PANEL

1 Make an artistic, collapsible wall panel from ¾-inch by 10-inch strips of 5-gauge clear acetate combined with straw sunbursts.
2 Staple 2 of the acetate strips together at both ends.
3 Do the same thing with another pair of strips. Now, staple the center of the bottom strip of the first pair to the center of the top strip of the second pair.
4 Continue until the desired length of panel is reached.
5 Cut ⅜-inch by 5-inch strips of the clear acetate. Staple one to each end of the pairs and at right angles to them. Also, staple one at each center where one pair joins another. Be sure that all these 5-inch strips project forward from the pairs.
6 Staple or sew a 3-inch straw sunburst onto the free tip of each 5-inch strip. (Back each straw sunburst with a colorful circle of felt if you wish.)
7 To keep the strips in the pairs uniformly spaced while hanging, punch a hole through the center of each strip and run a cord the full length of the panel. As the cord is being threaded through, slip 2 2¼-inch straws onto the cord between the 10-inch strips. (The stiffness of the straws will keep the strips uniformly spaced, and the break between the straws will allow the panel to be collapsed for storing when not in use.)

TREE DECORATION

1 Decorate a dense evergreen tree with tiny, white lights or with real candles.
2 Distribute dozens of straw sunbursts in various sizes over the surface of the tree.
3 Top the tree with a single large straw star. With no further decorations, the tree will be strikingly beautiful both day and night.

HOLIDAY CENTERPIECE

1 Mount straw sunbursts on the tips of straight wires of varying lengths by thrusting one wire into the open end of a single ray of each sunburst. Use number 21 florist's wire cut into 13-inch and 16-inch lengths. Use 9 of the long wires and 7 of the shorter ones.
2 Stick the free end of each wire into the narrow space between the candle and the candleholder. Distribute the sunbursts in a pleasing pattern around the candle.
3 Set the arrangement on a table covering of the same darkness or lightness as the wires. The sunbursts will appear to float in the candlelight. The straw takes on added glamour if the arrangement is placed under an overhead light.

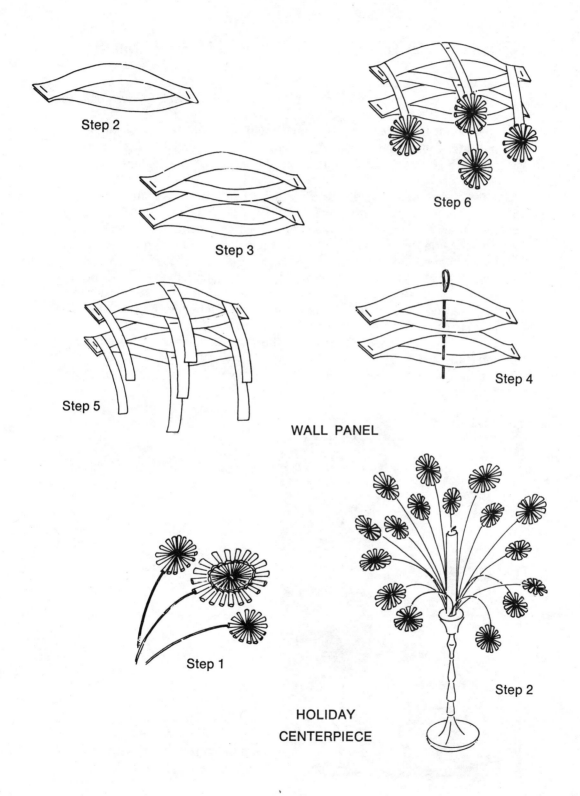

Step 2

Step 3

Step 6

Step 5

Step 4

WALL PANEL

Step 1

Step 2

HOLIDAY
CENTERPIECE

DECORATIVE TRIM ON STYROFOAM PYRAMIDS OR CONES

1 Select a styrofoam pyramid or cone and a suitable block of styrofoam for a base.
2 Spray both the base and the pyramid with gold finish. (Be sure the label indicates the spray is for use on styrofoam.)
3 Measure strips of straw to fit along the edges of the rectangular styrofoam base.
4 Miter the corners carefully, using a razor blade or very sharp scissors.
5 Pin or glue the strips into place.
6 Add straw sunburst ornaments to the base for accents.
7 Stretch wide rubber bands at 1-inch intervals up and down the styrofoam pyramid or cone.
8 Beginning at the top, slip selected dried magnolia leaves behind the first rubber band. Move down and do the same with each of the next bands. Each successive layer of leaves will cover the preceding rubber band and also stems of the preceding layer of leaves.
9 Tuck accents of straw sunbursts or other harmonizing plant materials into the leaf layers.
10 Pin finishing materials at the bottom to cover the last rubber band and bottom stems of the last row of leaves.

STYROFOAM PYRAMID
—STEPS 9 & 10.

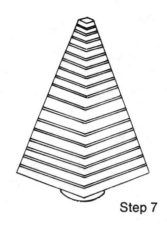

Step 7

Steps 5 & 6

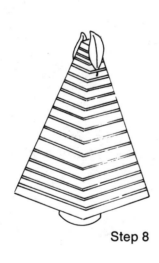

Step 8

STYROFOAM
PYRAMID

Steps 9 & 10

PERSONALIZED DECORATIVE PAPERS

Prepare your own decorative papers for gift wrappings and for linings or covers for gift boxes, using blueprint paper and straw sunburst stars. The process is amazingly simple and the results are delightful.

Secure blueprint paper from the company listed under Suppliers in this book or from a company nearer you. Huge sheets are available, but smaller ones will be cut at your request. Keep the blueprint paper in the dark until you are ready to make a print. Arrange straw sunbursts of various sizes on the light-sensitive side of the paper. Cover the work with a heavy paper and carry it to a sunny windless spot. On a windy day, place a glass over the straw figures and lay the heavy paper on top of the glass. In the sun, remove the heavy paper covering from the layout and expose the work for 30 seconds. Quickly remove a scattering of the stars and continue the exposure for another 30 seconds. (Exciting variations of dark and light that add depth to the composition are thus achieved.) Shake off the remaining stars and immerse the paper at once in clear water. Wash off the light-sensitive surface and lay the paper aside to dry. Finally, press the sheet with a warm iron or heavy book.

For added interest, work pressed ferns or weeds into the arrangement before blueprinting. Try other 2-dimensional forms such as the lacy sunburst and the 2-dimensional chicken in place of the small sunbursts.

LARGE LACY STAR

1 Prepare a large sunburst from 10 thick straws.
2 Insert long, thin strips of split straw into the open tips of the sunburst's rays.
3 Arch these strips to adjacent tips to form scalloped margins.
4 Develop many overlappings of the scallops at different levels to produce lovely lacy effects.
5 Gently pinch selected scallops to sharp points for added interest. Back the strips with masking tape if they seem inclined to break.
6 Telescope thin straws into the tips of the sunburst's rays with the split straws to prevent the scalloped straws from slipping out. Clip the thin straws off about 6 inches from the tips of the sunburst's rays. Save the scraps for more small sunbursts.

PERSONALIZED DECORATIVE PAPERS.

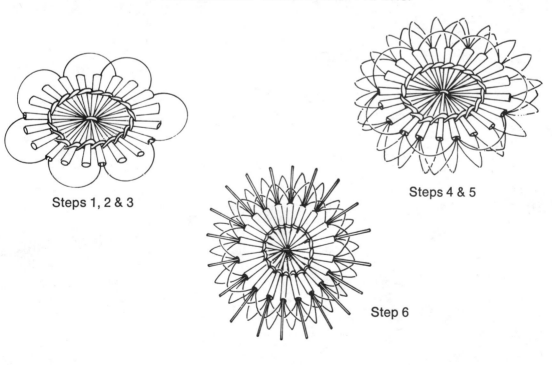

Steps 1, 2 & 3

Steps 4 & 5

Step 6

LARGE LACY STAR

HALF SUNBURSTS

1 Push a long, thin needle through the centers of 6 small, soaked straws to hold them while you tie.
2 Wrap a cord around the 6 straws close to the needle. Make the cord go across the top of the straws, then cross once underneath.
3 Hold the straws flat with a finger of one hand while you pull one end of the cord firmly and steadily with the other hand, making the straws fan into a half-circle. Tie a double knot in the cord. Snip off the excess. Remove the needle.
4 Space the straws by weaving in a cord.

These half sunbursts are used for combs on the French hen figures and, attached to wire stems, may serve as stylized flowers in dried-plant arrangements.

FLATTENED-STRAW SUNBURSTS

1 Lay 4 flattened, wet straws on top of each other in alternating positions.
2 Weave them together with a cord.
3 Lay 4 more straws underneath to fill in the spaces. Weave all 8 together. (The ends of the 8 straws produce a sunburst with 16 rays.)
4 Cut each ray to a long, sharp point.

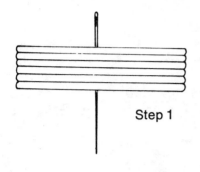

Step 1

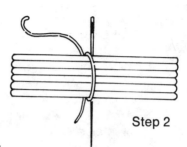

Step 2

HALF SUNBURST

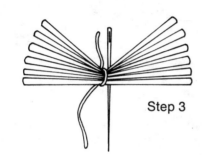

Step 3

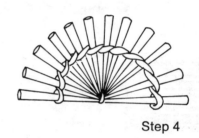

Step 4

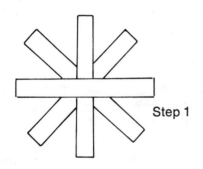

Step 1

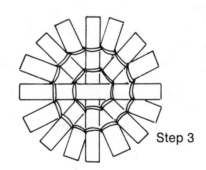

Step 3

FLATTENED STRAW SUNBURST

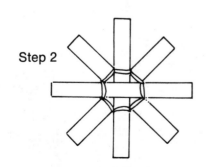

Step 2

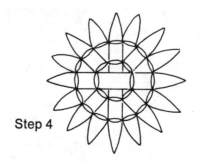

Step 4

STAR OF DAVID

1 Cut 6 thick straws 9½ inches long and 6 more straws 7 inches long. Soak the straws.
2 Tie 3 equal lengths of straw together at their tips to form an equilateral triangle. When you have used all 12 straws, you will have completed 4 separate triangles.
3 Arrange the 2 9½-inch triangles to form a 6-pointed star. Tie at their points of intersection.
4 Arrange the 2 7-inch triangles in the same manner and tie them at their points of intersection.
5 Fit the 2 stars together and tie them at all points of intersection. Notice that the 2 stars fit together more securely for tying if the corresponding triangles of the stars are not set together in the same order. If the triangle with the base upward is on top in the small star, then the triangle with the base upward in the large star should be turned so that it is on the bottom of that star.
6 Harmonize any ornamentation with the lines of the basic star form.

A straw sunburst may be cut to fit the hexagonal center or 2 ½-inch lengths of straw may be tied across intersections; cut all ends of these short straws to parallel the lines of the star.

Straw stars make attractive enrichments for dark wall panels or wall hangings. Laid flat on the table and centered with candlesticks, stars add a festive accent to holiday tables.

bird and animal figures

THE CHICKEN

The chicken motif may take either a 2-dimensional or a 3-dimensional form. Both forms utilize three of the basic techniques (tying, bending, and weaving) in their construction.

—TWO-DIMENSIONAL CHICKEN

1 Select straws of equal thicknesses. Cut 5 6-inch lengths.
2 Thrust a needle through all 5 wet straws at a point ¼ inch from one end of the bundle.

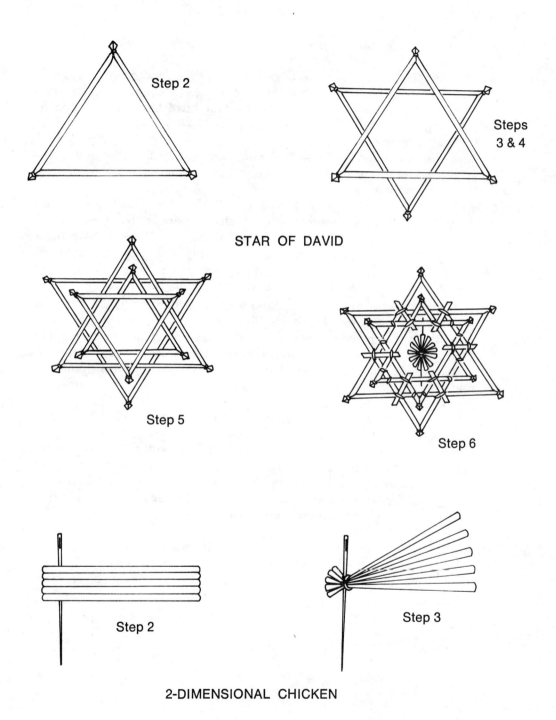

Step 2

Steps
3 & 4

STAR OF DAVID

Step 5

Step 6

Step 2

Step 3

2-DIMENSIONAL CHICKEN

3 Tie a cord close to the needle. (See Tying—Basic Techniques) Clip off excess cord and remove the needle.

4 With the thumbnail as a tool, begin bending the straws downward singly at a very sharp angle ¼ inch from the first tie. The bend on each straw should come only the thickness of the thumbnail beyond the bend in the previous straw. Continue this process until all 5 straws are bent. This makes the head of the chicken.

5 Push the top straws up to a slight peak, then insert the needle through all the straws at the neck line to hold them in place until a second tie has been completed.

6 To make the body, begin on the back of the chicken 1 inch down from the neck tie and make another series of sharp bends in the straws just as you did on the head but in the opposite direction. When all have been bent, push the front straws forward to give thickness to the body. Again, use the needle to hold the straws in position while you tie close to the needle. When the tie is finished, remove the needle.

7 To space the straws in the tail, loop a cord around the chicken's neck and tie a knot. Proceed to weave this cord around the tail-straws, using the weaving technique explained under Basic Techniques. Space the straws evenly, keeping the bottom straw of the tail in a line with the bottom of the chicken's body. Tie a knot in the cord at this point and snip off the ends. (Remove the weaving cord when the straws are dry.) Trim the tail-straws into an arc.

8 Make the legs from 2 5-inch straws that have number 21 florist's wire running the length of their hollow centers. Fold these straws in their middles and loop them over the chicken's back. Tie the 4 leg-straws together close beneath the body. Tie 2 of the straws together 1 inch down from the body for each leg. For the toes, bend 1 straw forward and 1 backward on each foot. Tie at the tips. Cut off extra straw and cord. (Use your nippers for cutting the wired straw. The wire will nick the edge of the scissors.)

9 Shape the beak by snipping it to a point with sharp scissors.

10 Split the top straw on the head lengthwise with a razor blade and insert a red flannel comb.

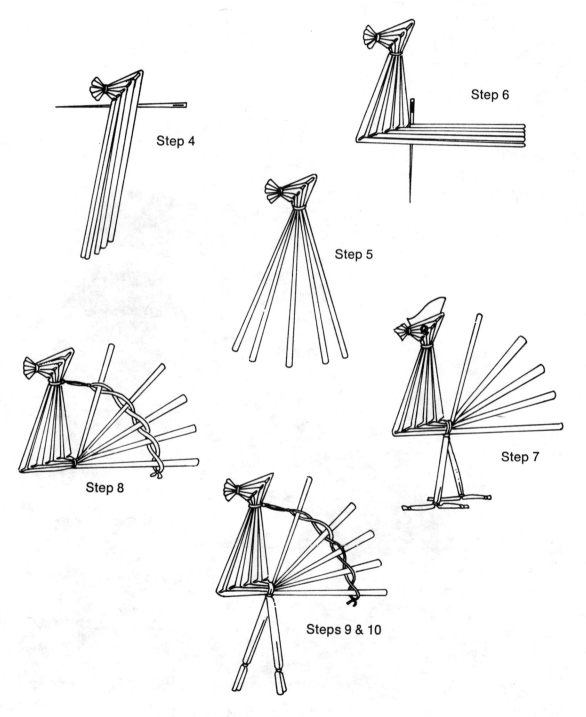

Step 4

Step 6

Step 5

Step 8

Step 7

Steps 9 & 10

2-DIMENSIONAL CHICKEN

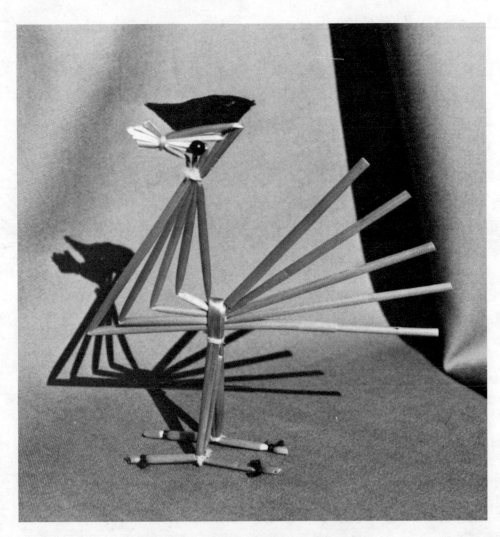

2-DIMENSIONAL STRAW CHICKEN.

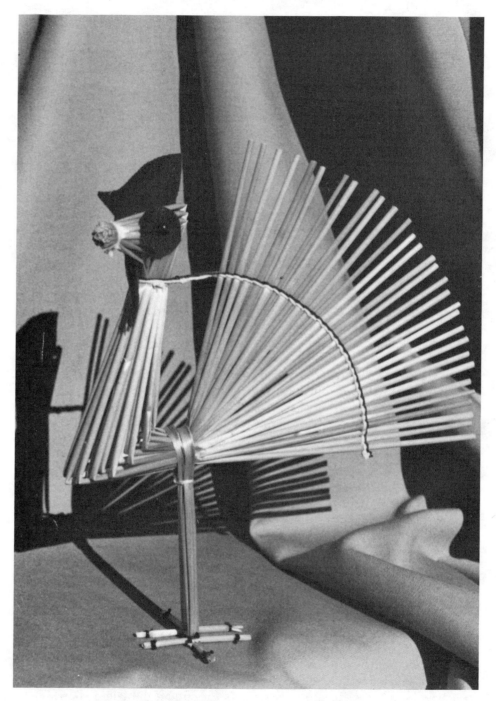

3-DIMENSIONAL STRAW CHICKEN.

—THREE-DIMENSIONAL CHICKEN

1 Select 30 long terminal straws of uniform thicknesses. The straws must be 12 to 15 inches long or longer. Put the thick ends of straws together at one end of the bundle.

2 Slip a small rubber band around this thick end of the bundle to hold while you tie very tightly ½ inch from that end. Clip off excess cord and remove the rubber band.

3 Holding the tied end with the left hand and using the right thumbnail as a tool, begin bending the straws downward singly at a very sharp angle ½ inch from the first tie. When the bends have been completed on the bottom layer of straws, start bending the straws on the next layer only the thickness of the thumbnail beyond the bends in the previous layer. Continue this bending process, moving out a small increment on each layer until the last straws, which form the top of the head, have been bent. When all the straws have been bent, push the topmost bends to a little peak and distribute the others evenly.

4 Slip a number 8 rubber band around the bundle at the neck line to hold while you tie the cord very tightly ⅛ inch below the bends in the bottom straws.

5 To make the body, begin on the back of the chicken 3 inches from the neck tie and make another series of bends as was done on the head but in the opposite direction. When all the straws have been bent, keep the back straws straight but push the front straws forward to give thickness to the body (about 2 inches). Distribute the other straws evenly.

6 Again use the small rubber band to hold while you make a firm tie about ¼ inch from the bend of the back straws.

7 To shape the tail, loop a long length of cord around the neck and tie a knot. Move out ¼ inch on the doubled cord and tie another knot. Using the weaving technique explained under Basic Techniques, space the tail-straws evenly and let the weaving cord hold them in place until dry. Later, a more colorful cord may be woven in and the original one removed. Try to keep the bottom straws of the tail in a straight line with the bottom body-straw.

8 Make the legs from 3 long straws that have number 21 florist's wires running the full length of their hollow centers. Fold these straws in the middle and loop them snugly over the chicken's back. Tie the 6 leg-straws together close beneath the body. Separate the straws to make 2 legs with 3 straws in each. Three inches below the body make a firm ankle tie on each leg. To make stylized feet, bend one straw forward, one backward, and one outside on each foot and tie each toe near its tip. (Each toe should be about 1 inch long.) Snip off excess cord and straw. Remember to use your nippers for cutting the wired straw.

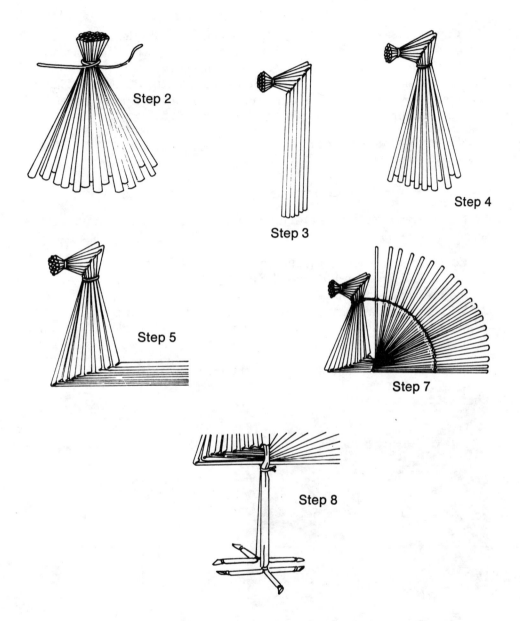

Step 2

Step 3

Step 4

Step 5

Step 7

Step 8

3-DIMENSIONAL CHICKEN

9 Clip the beak to a sharpened cone shape. Trim the tail into an artistic arc about 4½ inches from the body tie. (Save all scraps of straw to use in making sunbursts or glued-straw pictures.)
10 Stick a black map tack into a circle of red flannel for each eye. Shape a piece of red flannel for a comb and push it into a straw that has been split lengthwise to receive it.

For colorful accents, 2-ply red yarn may be used to cover the ecru cord ties and to replace the ecru cord in the tail.

—THREE FRENCH HENS

With some variation in its attire, the chicken sculpture may take on a festive air and become a French Hen.

1 Construct a 3-dimensional chicken. Omit the red trim.
2 Replace the ecru cord in the tail with metallic cord and the circle around the eye with a large metallic sequin.
3 Wire 3 small straw sunbursts to the tail above the woven cord.
4 Wire to the top of the head a half-sunburst (see construction details under The Sunburst in this section).

Three French hens standing together create a pleasing rhythmic unit.

FRENCH HEN.

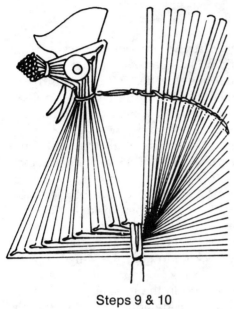

3-DIMENSIONAL
CHICKEN

Steps 9 & 10

FRENCH
HEN

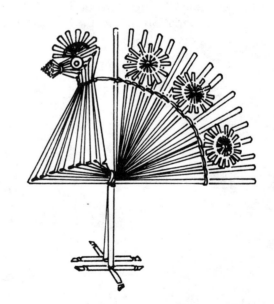

FLYING BIRD

1 Construct the wings first. Select 8 soaked straws of medium thickness and 5 inches in length. Lay these straws side by side on a flat surface and push a needle through their centers to hold while you tie. Pull the cord tightly so that the straws fan out in both directions. Tie a firm knot and clip off the ends of the cord. Trim the wing straws into a neat curve from 2½ inches on the top straw to 1¼ inches on the bottom straw.

2 The head, body, and tail are all made in one piece. Use 11 straws of the same thickness and length as for the wings. Tie all 11 together ½ inch from their tips to make the beak. Trim to a point.

3 One-fourth inch from the tie, make a sharp bend in each of the 5 top straws. Push these straws forward slightly so that they make a ridge for the top of the head. Tie them in that position to the 6 bottom straws.

4 Insert the center of the wing piece between the 5 top straws and 6 bottom straws. Tie again ¾ inch from the neck tie to hold the wings in place and to make the body.

5 Shape the 11 tail-straws so that they curve up in the middle. Clip them to form a swallow tail 3½ inches long at the outside and 2¼ inches long in the middle.

6 Attach a cord at the body tie for hanging.

7 A variation of this bird figure is shown in the accompanying illustration.

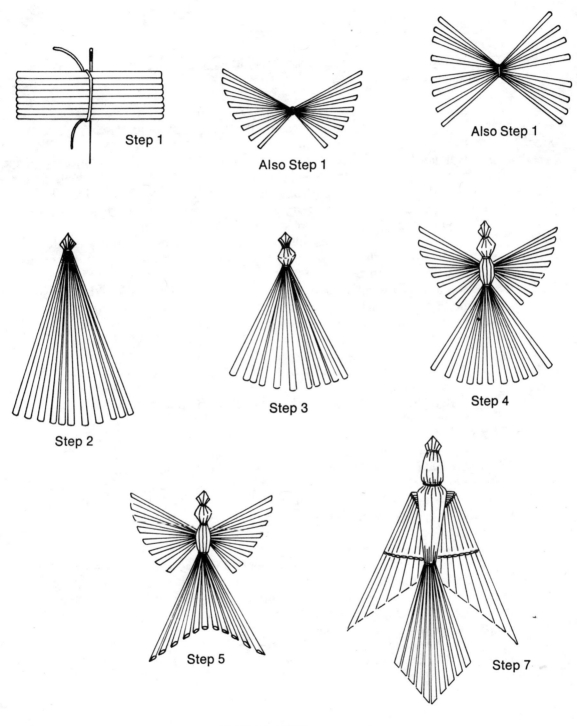

Step 1

Also Step 1

Also Step 1

Step 2

Step 3

Step 4

Step 5

Step 7

FLYING BIRD

THE GOAT

The goat figure uses 3 of the basic techniques (tying, bending, and braiding) in its construction.

1 Select 30 long, soaked straws of uniform thickness.

2 Slip a small rubber band around the bundle to hold it while you tie tightly ½ inch from the end to form the nose.

3 Holding the nose portion with the left hand and using the thumbnail of the right hand as a tool, begin bending the straws downward singly at a very sharp angle ½ inch from the first tie. When the bends have been completed on the bottom layer of straws, start bending the straws on the next layer just the thickness of the thumbnail beyond the bend in the previous layer. Continue this bending process, moving out a small increment on each layer until the last straws, which form the top of the head, have been bent.

4 Slip a rubber band around the bundle at the neck line to hold while you tie the cord very tightly ⅛ inch below the bend in the bottom straws.

5 Measure down 2 inches from the tie at the back of the neck and do another series of sharp bends on 20 of the middle straws. Leave 5 of the straws unbent on each side of the body for front legs.

6 Slip a small rubber band around the 20 bent straws to hold while you tie a cord close to the bend in the straws. (The cord should not be pulled very tightly here; also, the rubber band may be left on to help hold, then snipped off later.)

7 Tie 5 of the unbent straws into each front leg. Make the tie 2½ inches down from the body.

8 To increase the thickness of the body and the back legs, wrap 4 more long, thick straws around the front of the body and let them extend back to be used with the 20 body-straws for constructing the back legs. Tie these straws to the body, once near the front legs and again near the back legs.

9 Beginning on the underside of the body 2 inches from the front legs, bend all but the top 3 straws downward one at a time to form the back legs. Half of these bent straws go into each back leg. Tie the legs at the ankle line 2½ inches down from the body. Clip off the bottom straws of the 4 legs evenly so that the figure will stand alone.

10 Beginning at the hip joint, braid the 3 unbent back-straws to make the tail. Tie the tip. Clip off excess straw and cord. Shape the tail into a curved line while it is still damp. Use a paper clip or bobby pin to hold it in shape until it is dry.

Step 1   Step 2

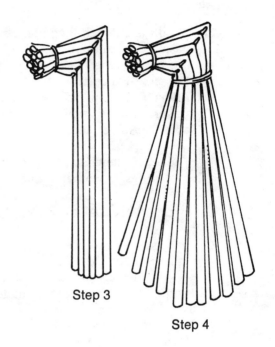

Step 3

Step 4

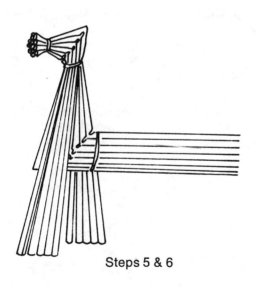

Steps 5 & 6

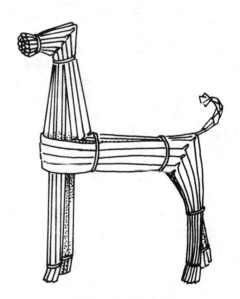

Steps 7, 8, 9 & 10

THE GOAT

11 Braid the 2 5-inch-long horns separately following the instructions under Basic Techniques for braiding 3 straws. Tie these on opposite sides of the head at the neck line. Roll them backward into curved lines while they are still damp.

12 Add a black map tack on each side of the head for eyes.

13 Cover leg and body ties with ¼-inch velvet ribbon to provide festive accents. Add a piece of grain head for a small beard if you wish.

The same general plan used for the goat and chicken figures can be followed to fashion other animals and birds.

OTHER ANIMALS AND BIRDS

1 The giraffe is made with a longer and more slender neck than the goat figure and has short lengths of flattened, wet straw wrapped around the neck at intervals and tied close to the neck in the back.

2 The pony also has a mane made from short lengths of straw and tied at the back of the neck.

3 The sheep has a woolly coat and tail made from grain heads tied and glued to the body-straws.

4 The mane and tail of the horse figure are also made from grain heads.

5 The squirrel's tail is made from a cluster of grain heads that have been wired and shaped.

6 The rabbit's head and back have some straws plaited to help develop the rounded shapes.

7 The stork's wings and legs are made separately, then folded in their middles and slipped into the body-straws before the tie is made for the tail.

8 The parrot is made in a similar fashion, except that the wings are simply an extension of the head-straws.

9 The sitting chicken is made from cornhusks and veneered with a final layer of straw husks that have been turned inside out to reveal the glossy underneath surface. Like the other bird figures, construction begins by

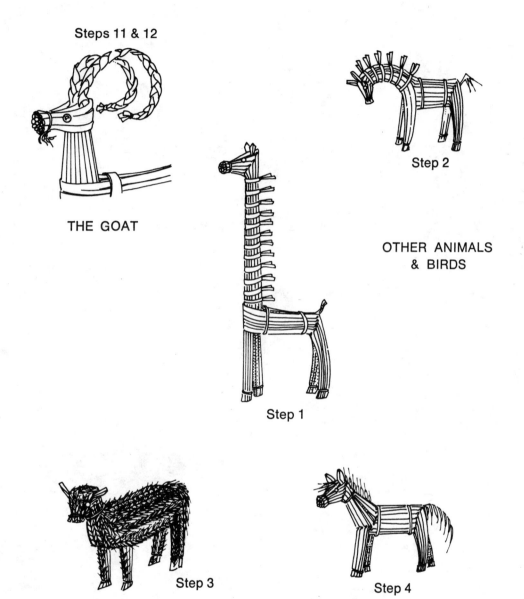

Steps 11 & 12

THE GOAT

Step 2

OTHER ANIMALS
& BIRDS

Step 1

Step 3

Step 4

Step 5

Step 7

Step 6

Step 8

Step 9

OTHER ANIMALS
& BIRDS

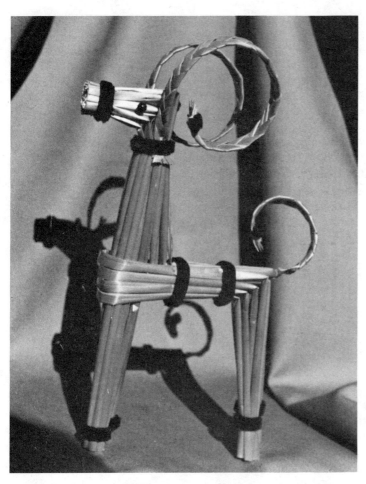

STRAW GOAT FIGURE.

SITTING CHICKEN—OTHER ANIMALS AND BIRDS—STEP 9.

tying at the beak, then moving to the neck tie and finally the body tie. The eye section is a unique feature. A cornhusk folded at both edges and rolled into a tight coil is inserted into the center of the head bundle before the neck tie is made. A pipe cleaner laid in each of the two folds before the husk is rolled up gives extra thickness to the eye coils. A map tack pushed into the center of each end of the coil completes the eyes.

angel and child figures

THE ANGEL

1   For the head use a 10mm natural wood bead (see Suppliers) into which you have pushed a small wooden dowel or matchstick, about 1½ inches long. The dowel makes a neck and a foundation to which the body-straws will be attached.

2   To prepare the arms, select 2 thin straws 2 inches long. Push straight number 21 wires through the entire lengths of their hollow centers. Using fine gold wire instead of cord, tie the straws together at the center and at the wrist lines. Bend at the shoulder and elbow lines.

3   For the wings, select 10 2½-inch, thin, soaked straws. Construct the wings by following instructions for making the sunburst (Basic Techniques—Tying and Weaving), but weave the cord into the two halves separately. Space the straws evenly and trim each wing into a graceful curve from 1¼ inches long at the top to 1 inch at the bottom. After the straws have dried, replace the ecru cord with gold cord. Wire the ends of the gold cord together to avoid a bulky tie. (If you are making several angels, prepare a supply of heads, arms, and wings ahead of time.)

4   For the body, choose 25 3-inch long, thin, wet straws. Slip the wooden dowel of the head down into one end of the bundle. Hold all together with a rubber band. Wrap a cord around twice at the neck line ¼ inch from the ends of the straws. Pull very tightly and tie securely. Bend the ¼-inch ruff down sharply over the tie-string before proceeding. (This prevents straws from pulling out.)

5   Slip the center of the arm piece into the center of the bundle just below the neck tie. Position the wings at the back and bring the 2 center-back straws down over the center-tie of the wings. Push the wings and arms up as close to the neck tie as they will go. Hold all in place with a rubber band while you tie as closely as possible below the arms and wings.

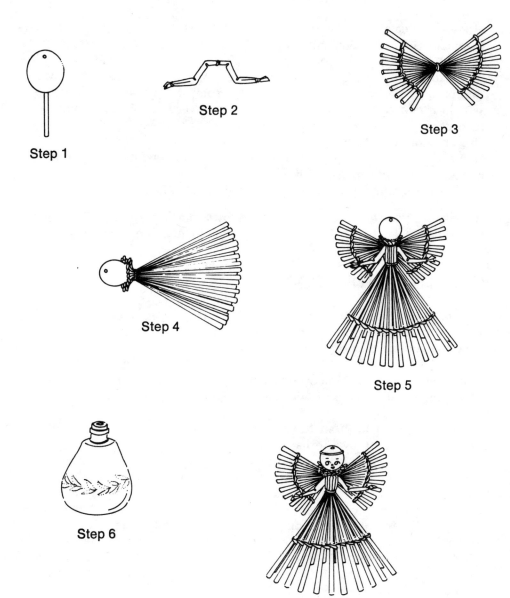

Step 1

Step 2

Step 3

Step 4

Step 5

Step 6

Steps 7 & 8

THE ANGEL

6 Using the weaving technique (Basic Techniques), shape the skirt into a complete circle. Position the skirt to dry over a small, round salt shaker (about 1¾ inches in diameter by 2¼ inches high), inserting the dowel of the head-piece into the hole in the shaker. Slip a wide rubber band over the top of the head and down over the bottom of the shaker to hold the skirt in a taut circle overnight while it dries. Weave a 16-inch length of gold cord into the skirt to replace the ecru cord when the straw is dry. Use fine gold wire to hold the ends of the gold cord together.

7 Shape a 1-inch length of gold cord into a halo by wrapping it around a pencil; then glue it on top of the head.

8 Finally, clip off any excess straw in the ruff around the neck.

A striking circular unit can be created by arranging a group of these angels around a lighted candle with the candlelight casting long shadows outward.

THE ORNAMENTED POD

Straw figures mounted inside clean, dry milkweed pods are pleasingly decorative. Experiment with tiny straw sunbursts and animal or plant forms. I will describe the construction of a child figure as ornamentation.

1 Gather clean, unstained milkweed pods. Allow them to dry. If a pod needs reshaping, wet it and stuff it with tissue paper to hold it in the shape desired until it has dried.

2 Make a sunburst halo from 10 very thin, 1-inch-long, wet straws. Cut this sunburst into a long oval to harmonize with the shape of the pod. Using a needle threaded with fine gold wire, attach this halo to the inside of the pod with a loop of the wire inserted from the outside back of the pod.

3 Make the head by inserting a matchstick or small wooden dowel into an 8mm natural wood bead (see Suppliers). The stick holds the head and also provides a foundation upon which to tie the body-straws.

4 Make the arms by running number 21 florist's wire through the hollow centers of 2 1-inch-long straws. Tie them together with fine gold wire at their centers and wrist lines. (Prepare a supply of heads and arms ahead of time if you plan to make several figures.)

5 Select 6 wet straws 2 or 2½ inches long, depending upon the length of the pod, for the construction of the body. Tie these to the dowel at the neck line. Slip the arms into place behind 5 of the straws. Push these arms up as close as possible to the neck tie and secure them in place by wrapping fine gold wire below them at the waistline.

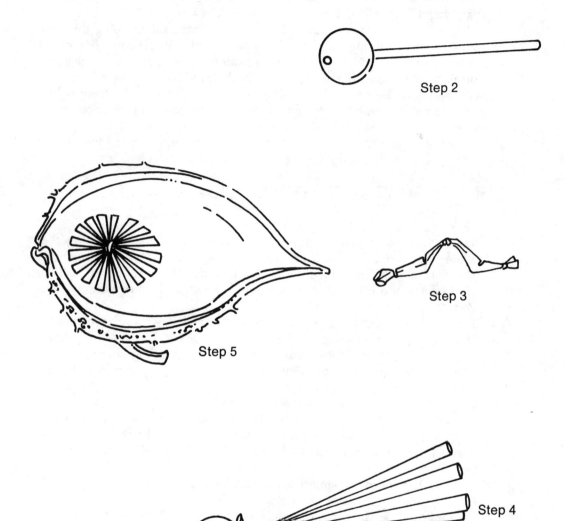

Step 2

Step 3

Step 5

Step 4

THE ORNAMENTED POD

6 For the lower part of the body, keep 1 back straw straight, but make a sharp bend in each of the 5 front straws. Try to make the bends form a shallow V-shape rather than a straight line. Then, still keeping the back straw straight, push the front straws up until the bends assume an angle of about 110 degrees. Tie them in this position to the back straw near the bottom, using fine gold wire. Wrap the body (as illustrated) with gold cord.

7 Sew the figure into place by passing a thin wire through the back of the pod, around the waist of the figure, and out the back of the pod. Twist the ends of the wire together and nip off the excess.

8 To complete the ornament, glue a strip of gold sequins around the margin of the pod. Attach a loop of wire to the stem for hanging.

CHILD FIGURE WITH TUNIC AND CAP

1 Select 25 thin soaked straws 4½ inches long.

2 Slip a small rubber band around the bundle to hold the straws together while you make a firm tie with cord ½ inch from the tip of the bundle. The cord should be pulled so tightly that the straws under it will be crushed and the rest of the bundle will fan out in all directions.

3 Trim the tops of the straws to a point.

4 Turn the bundle upside down and bend all straws downward over the tie.

5 Make a second tie ¾ inches down from the first tie to form the head. The concealed tips of the straws now provide padding to fill out the head, and the trimmed tips allow the cord to pull the straws in to form a neck at the second tie.

6 To make the arms, select 3 straws 3 inches long. Push straight number 21 wires through the entire lengths of their hollow centers. These wires allow the arms to hold their positions after they are bent. Tie the arm-straws together at their tips to form wrists. Make ties for the elbows ¾ inch from the wrist ties.

7 Insert the center of the length of arm-straws into the center of the bundle of body-straws just below the neck tie.

8 To hold the arms in that position, tie a cord ⅝ inch below the neck tie at the waistline.

9 From the center of the 25 straws extending downward from the waist line, sort out 8 straws for legs. Slip a small rubber band around them to hold while you work with the remaining 17 straws.

10 One and one-half inches down from the neck tie clip off the bottoms of the 17 straws to make a tunic-length garment.

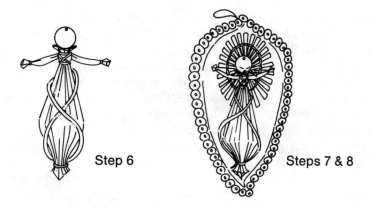

Step 6

Steps 7 & 8

THE ORNAMENTED POD

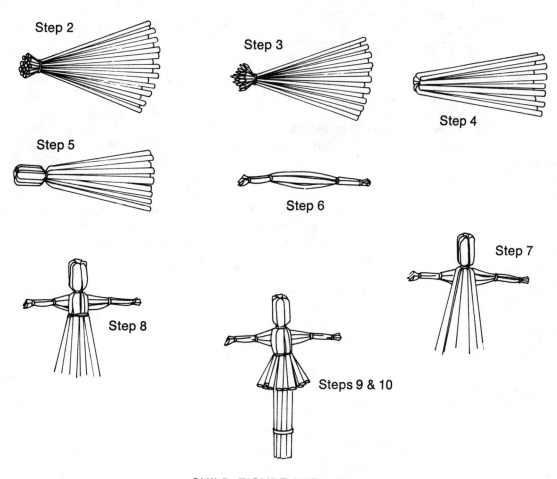

Step 2

Step 3

Step 4

Step 5

Step 6

Step 7

Step 8

Steps 9 & 10

CHILD FIGURE WITH TUNIC

11 Continue with the legs by separating the 8 long straws into 2 bundles of 4 straws each. Push a number 21 wire into the hollow center of 1 or more straws in each leg group. Tie each leg bundle near its tip. Move upward ⅝ inch from the first ties and tie again to form ankles. Again move upward and make knee ties ¾ inch from the ankle ties.

12 To complete the tunic, fold 2 2½-inch straws into inverted U-shapes and slip one over each shoulder. Secure these by passing a red cord around them and tying them to the waist.

13 Make a small pointed cap from red flannel. The finished cap should measure ¾ inch in front and 1¼ inches in the seamed back. The back seam and bottom hem should be turned to the inside. Attach a 5-inch loop of red cord at the peak of the cap for hanging.

14 Use small flat-headed black tacks for eyes and mouth.

15 Last, bend the arms at the elbow ties; bend the feet at the ankle ties; bend the knees slightly.

SKATING FIGURES

A pair of skaters may be made following the same plan outlined for the child figure with a few variations.

1 To make joined arms for the skaters, use 3 straws 6 inches long. Push a number 21 wire through the entire length of at least one hollow center. Tie the 3 straws into a circle by overlapping the ends, then tying. Insert this circle of straws into the centers of the two bundles of body-straws below the neck lines just before you tie at the waistlines. Let the tied end be hidden in one of the bundles of body-straws. Shape the circle to make shoulders for the two figures. Tie at the wrist lines with red cord.

2 Cut off below the knee line the 17 straws left for the tunic and tie them to the legs to form knickers.

3 Bend the legs into a skating position.

4 Attach the feet to a small piece of cardboard or wood to make the skaters stand.

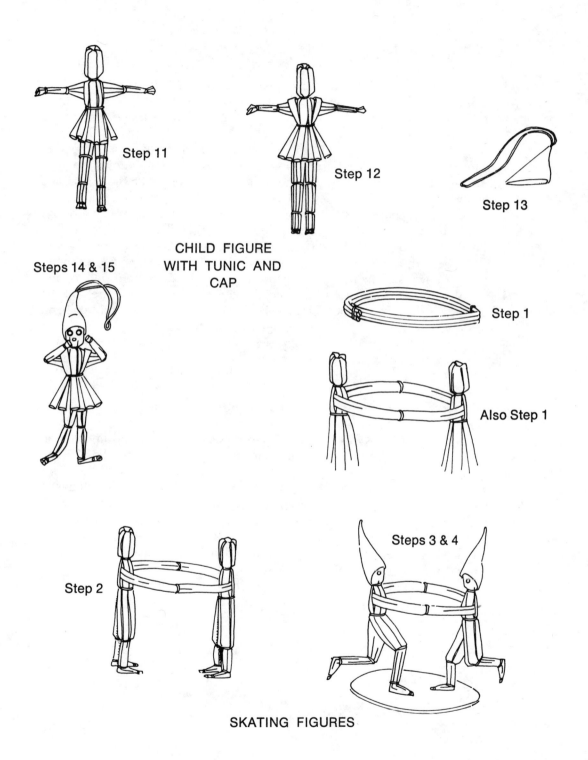

Step 11

Step 12

Step 13

CHILD FIGURE
WITH TUNIC AND
CAP

Steps 14 & 15

Step 1

Also Step 1

Step 2

Steps 3 & 4

SKATING FIGURES

PEASANT GIRL

1 For the head use a 10mm natural wood bead (see Suppliers) into which you have pushed a small wooden dowel about 1½ inches long. This dowel makes the neck and a foundation to which the body-straws will be attached.

2 For the arms, select 4 thin, soaked straws 3 inches long. Push a number 21 wire into the hollow center of at least one straw. The wire allows the arms to stay bent in a position. Tie the arm-straws together at the wrists and elbow lines.

3 For the body, choose 33 thin straws 3 inches long. Slip the wooden dowel of the head down into one end of the bundle. Hold all together with a small rubber band. Wrap a cord around twice at the neck line ¼ inch from the ends of the straws. Pull very tightly and tie with a firm knot. Bend the ruff down sharply over the tie cord to prevent straws from pulling out.

4 Slip the center of the arm piece into the center of the bundle behind the dowel and just below the neck tie. Hold all in place with a rubber band while you tie beneath the arms ½ inch below the neck tie.

5 Look into the end of the bundle of 33 straws. Sort out 8 straws from the center of the bundle and slip a rubber band around them. Push the remaining 25 straws up sharply at the waist line to provide space for tying the leg-straws.

6 Tie 4 of the straws from the center of the bundle into each leg after inserting a wire into the hollow center of at least one straw in each leg group. First tie near the tips of the straws, then move up ⅝ inch and tie again at the ankle lines. Move up another ¾ inch and tie at the knee lines. Bend at the ankle lines to form feet.

7 Cut off about 1½ inches from the bottoms of the 25 remaining straws to make a skirt. Use lengths of colored cord or 2-ply yarn to weave a gay border design into the bottom of the skirt. (See weaving instructions under Basic Techniques.)

8 Make yarn braids and a tiny flannel hood for the head. A piece of the same flannel may be used for a shawl.

9 Attach the feet to a cardboard or wooden circle to make the figure stand.

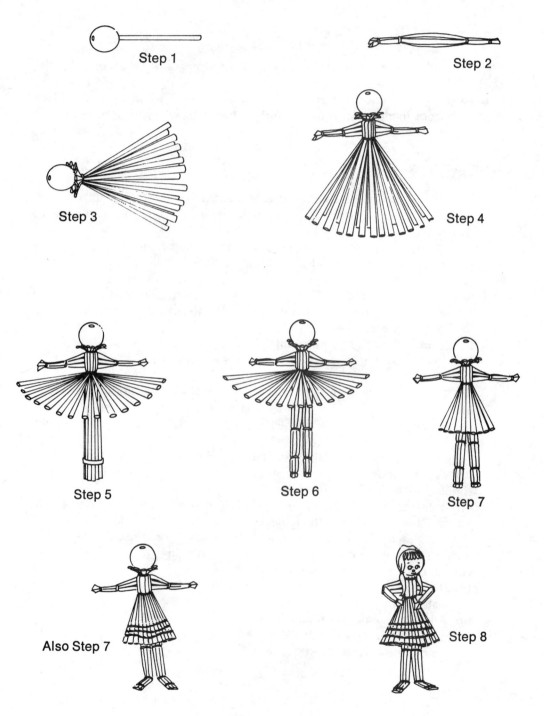

Step 1

Step 2

Step 3

Step 4

Step 5

Step 6

Step 7

Also Step 7

Step 8

PEASANT GIRL

LADY WITH BROOM

The lady with the broom is made exactly like the peasant girl except that the skirt is left full length and legs may be omitted.

To complete, tie a small triangular scarf onto the head. In her hand, place a small broom made from a thin wooden dowel to which a bundle of very thin straws has been tied.

LARGE ANGEL

1   For the head, use a ¾-inch wooden bead into which a small wooden dowel has been pushed. The dowel serves as a neck and as a base to which body-straws will be tied.

2   Push the neck dowel into the center of a bundle of 48 6-inch straws.

3   Slip a rubber band around to hold all together while you tie tightly ½ inch from the ends of the straws. Pull the ruff down sharply over the tie to prevent straws from pulling out. If you wish to eliminate the ruff, tie the 48 straws to the neck dowel with the head pointed downward. Then turn the bundle upside down and pull all the long ends down over the tie to cover the cord and the ruff.

4   For the arms, tie together near their tips 4 6-inch lengths of straw that have had number 21 wire run through their hollow centers. Move out 1½ inches from these first ties and tie again at the elbow lines.

5   Make wings from 11 17-inch straws. Lay them side by side on a flat surface. Insert a long needle at their centers and tie, following instructions for Tying under Basic Techniques.

6   Beginning ½ inch from the tie, start a series of sharp bends following instructions under Bending—Basic Techniques. The bend in the last straw should be about 1½ inches from the tie.

7   Beginning at the last bend, weave a double cord into the wings at the bends. Then, without cutting the cord, turn and weave another row at right angles to the first line of weaving, ending on the outside of the wings 2¼ inches from the end of the previous line of weaving. Tie the cord and clip off excess ends.

8   Insert the center of the arm-straws into the center of the bundle of 48 body-straws just below the neck tie.

9   Bring 4 of the center back-straws down over the center of the wings.

10   One inch down from the neck tie, make a snug tie at the waist line to hold the arms and wings in position.

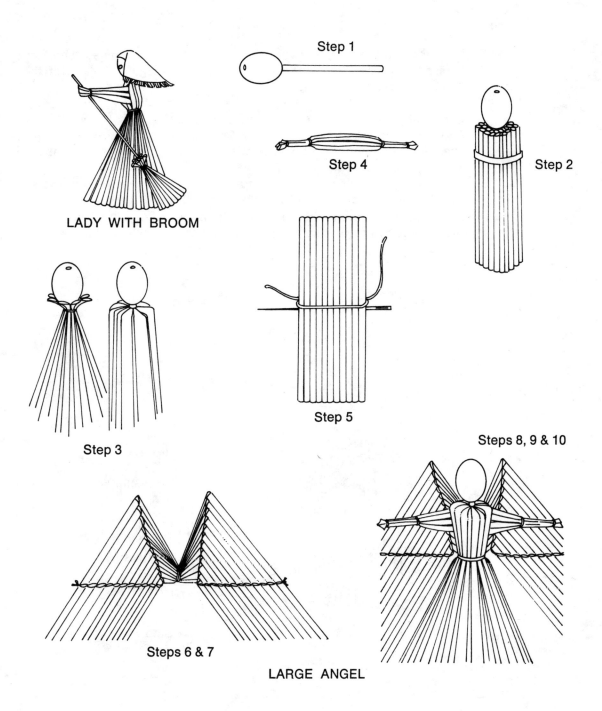

LADY WITH BROOM

Step 1

Step 4

Step 2

Step 3

Step 5

Steps 8, 9 & 10

Steps 6 & 7

LARGE ANGEL

11 Bend the end straws of the wings downward one at a time so that each is in a vertical position. Taper the ends to a 45-degree angle with the short ends nearest the body.

12 To hold the tips of the wings in that position, thread 2 long cords through the center back of the skirt 1 inch down from the waist line. Allow the ends to extend in both right and left directions from the body. Then weave them across the 11 straws of the wings and tie them at the outer edges.

13 Bend the arms downward at the shoulder line and bend the elbows so that the forearms are in a vertical position with hands upward.

14 Weave a gold cord into the skirt 1 inch from the bottom and fit the figure over a bottle to dry. Make a halo from gold cord for the head.

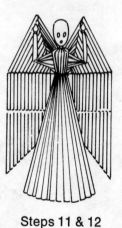

Steps 11 & 12

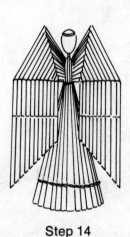

Step 14

LARGE ANGEL

CHILD FIGURE WITH TUNIC AND CAP—
STEPS 14 & 15.

LARGE ANGEL—STEP 14.

threaded-straw designs

SPATIAL FORMS

The open spatial forms are constructed from dry straws, using only one of the basic techniques, threading. Review Threading under Basic Techniques before beginning.

1 Thread 4 equal lengths of straw together to form a square.
2 From the corners of the square, thread straws above and below to form open pyramid shapes. To prevent the cord from splitting the straws, cut separate short lengths of cord and tie at all intersections.
3 Fasten these units (made in many sizes) together to form enchantingly complex mobile structures. The ever-changing relationships of moving, suspended forms provide constant interest for the observer.

THE ICOSAHEDRON

A somewhat more complex spatial form can be constructed using the same basic technique. This structure is made up of 20 equilateral triangles and is called by mathematicians an icosahedron.

1 Cut 40 dry straws of the same lengths and thicknesses.
2 Thread 20 together to form a central zone of 10 triangles. Join the two ends of this zone of triangles together.
3 From the vertices of these central triangles, thread 5 straws above and 5 below to complete the icosahedron.
4 Tie at all points of intersection.
5 Construct 20 straw sunbursts to fit the 20 triangles of the icosahedron.
6 Insert a long, thin straw into the hollow centers of one top and one bottom ray of each sunburst. Wire or tie these to the vertex and base of each triangular facet of the icosahedron. Clip off the excess ends of the thin straws after securing them.
7 Suspend the finished spatial form from a gold cord.

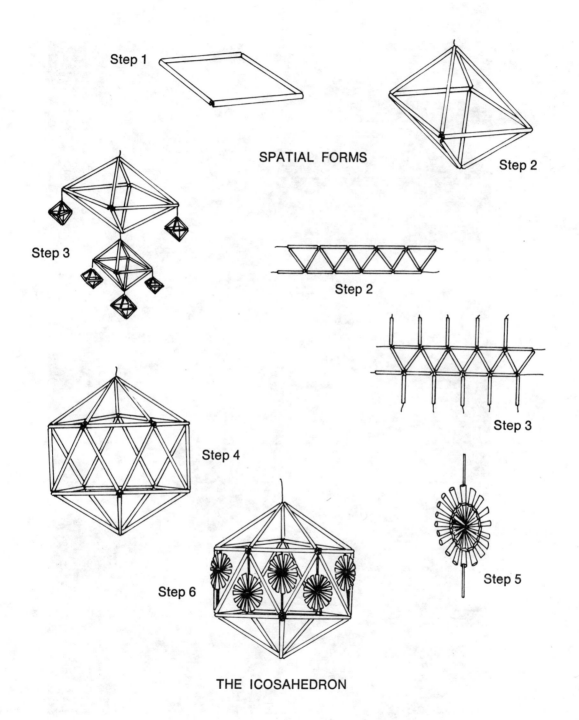

Step 1

SPATIAL FORMS

Step 2

Step 3

Step 2

Step 3

Step 4

Step 5

Step 6

THE ICOSAHEDRON

ICOSAHEDRON ORNAMENTED WITH STRAW SUNBURSTS.

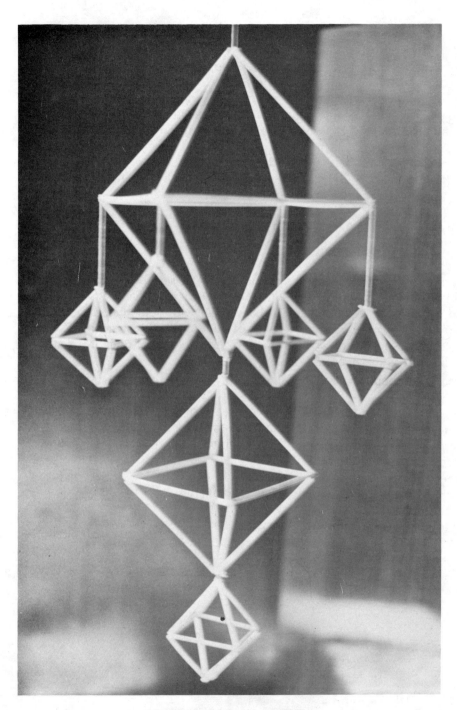

SPATIAL FORMS—STEP 3.

THREADED-STRAW EARRINGS

1 Procure a pair of drop-style earclips (see Suppliers).
2 Wire a ¾-inch length of small chain to the eyelet of each earring.
3 Cut 32 1½-inch-long straws (16 for each earring).
4 Thread each straw by running a thread through its hollow center, through a small bead, then back through the hollow center of the straw. (The bead should be large enough not to slip back through the hole of the straw.) Prepare each of the 32 straws in this way before proceeding.
5 Tie 16 of these threaded straws to the links of each suspended chain, distributing them carefully from top to bottom.

THREADED-STRAW ROOM DIVIDER
OR WINDOW BEAUTIFIER

1 Cut a quantity of dry straws of various thicknesses into lengths ranging from 4 to 6 inches. Purchase a supply of ¼-inch wooden beads in natural wood color or in a color that will harmonize with your décor.
2 Make a needle from a straight length of number 21 florist's wire. The eye of the needle must be very narrow and the wire quite straight, or straws will be split as the needle passes through them.
3 Thread the needle with lightweight cord that has been cut into the desired lengths.
4 Tie a large knot in the end of the cord and thread it through one of the ¼-inch beads. Then thread it through a length of straw and another bead. Alternate beads and straws until the desired length is reached.
5 Remove the end of the cord from the needle and tie it firmly to a wooden dowel or curtain rod.
6 Make as many strands as are needed to fill the width being decorated. Space strands about 1 inch apart. Arrange the beads in interesting patterns rather than have them occur in straight lines across the hanging.

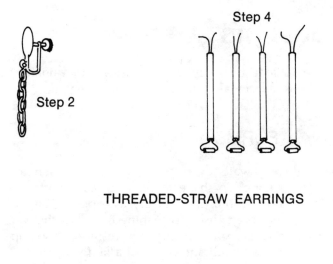

Step 4

Step 2

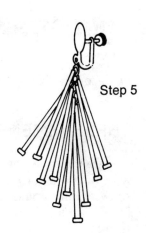

Step 5

THREADED-STRAW EARRINGS

Step 1

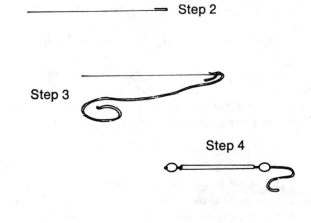

Step 2

Step 3

Step 4

Step 6

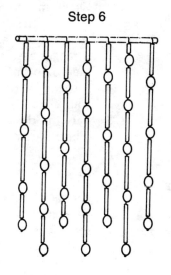

**THREADED-STRAW
ROOM DIVIDER, ETC.**

split-straw designs

Split straws have an almost metallic luster. They lend themselves to a number of decorative uses, both as 3-dimensional forms and as ornamentation for flat surfaces.

THREE-DIMENSIONAL FORMS

Prepare the straws by soaking them in water overnight. Split the straws lengthwise with a razor blade or sharp knife. To shape them, wrap each flattened straw around a glass and tie or tape it into place to dry as explained under Basic Techniques. A quicker way to accomplish this shaping is to iron the wet strip flat with a warm iron and then to relax, or curl, the resulting dry strip by drawing several times between the thumb and blade of a knife or scissors. Be sure to have the blade on the under side of the straw strip. This technique will produce a smooth curve free from kinks. After the straw strip has been made pliable, shape it into a tighter coil by winding it smoothly around a pencil or small wooden dowel.

—OPEN-SPHERE DESIGNS

1   Cut from 3 to 5 ⅛-inch-wide strips of 8-inch-long split straws.
2   Make circles from these strips by gluing the two ends of each together with white glue.
3   Arrange these circles to form an open sphere. Glue the circles together at their points of intersection.
4   Suspend interesting, related forms inside the sphere or decorate the top with a small straw sunburst.
5   Vary the design by assembling 3 spheres of different sizes inside of each other. Glue them together at their tops and attach a cord for hanging.

—SPLIT-STRAW EARRINGS

1   For each earring, cut an 11½-inch length of ⅜-inch-wide split straw.
2   Relax the strip by passing it several times between your thumb and a scissors blade. Be sure the blade is next to the under side of the strip.
3   Coil it into 3 circles with graded diameters of 1 inch, 1¼ inches, and 1½ inches. Push these circles together at one point on their circumferences and glue them in that position.
4   Thread a thin gold wire through a ½-inch wooden bead, on through a small pearl or glass bead, and back through the wooden bead.
5   Push the two ends of the wire through the eye of a needle and sew it through the point at which the 3 circles are glued. Remove the needle

**3-DIMENSIONAL
FORMS**

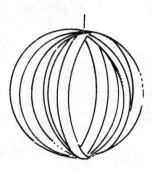

**OPEN SPHERE
DESIGNS**

Step 4

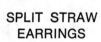

Step 3

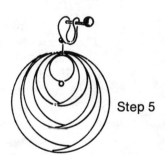

Step 5

**SPLIT STRAW
EARRINGS**

and fasten the ends of the wire to the eyelet of a drop-style earclip. Leave a little space so that the coil and bead can float freely.

—SMALL BIRD FIGURES

1 Select a straw that will fit the hole in a ½-inch natural wooden bead. Make a diagonal slash in one end of the straw to form a beak. Push the other end into the hole of the bead and glue it into place.
2 Glue the head bead to the hole of a ⅝-inch wooden bead. This completes the head and body of a small bird.
3 For the tail, wrap a 4-inch length of ⅜-inch split straw around the body bead and cross it at the lower back. Glue it together in a V-shape and attach it to the body bead with another daub of glue. Cut the ends to form a simplified swallow tail.
4 For the wings, taper the ends of a 5-inch by ⅜-inch split straw to long points. Wrap the center of this wing strip around the body and glue it into place.
5 Push a straw into the hole at the base of the body bead and glue a 1½-inch length of ¼-inch dowel at right angles to it to serve as a perch.
6 Make the figure stand by inserting the bottom end of the long straw into the center of a spool.

Another bird form may be made from strips of flattened straw glued into shapes for body, head, and beak and assembled as illustrated.

—STYLIZED TREE

1 Cut 3 strips of split straw 3½ inches by ⅜ inch.
2 Relax these straws by passing each between the thumb and a scissors blade.
3 Glue the ends of each together at right angles.
4 Arrange the 3 shaped pieces back to back and glue them to a 4-inch length of small wooden dowel, ½ inch from its end.
5 Prepare another group of 3 shaped pieces using 3-inch lengths of split straw and glue them to the dowel back to back ¾ inch below the previous group.
6 Construct a third group of 3 shaped pieces from 2½-inch lengths of split straw. Glue them to the dowel back to back ¾ inch below the second group.
7 For hanging, provide the top of the dowel with a small eye screw.

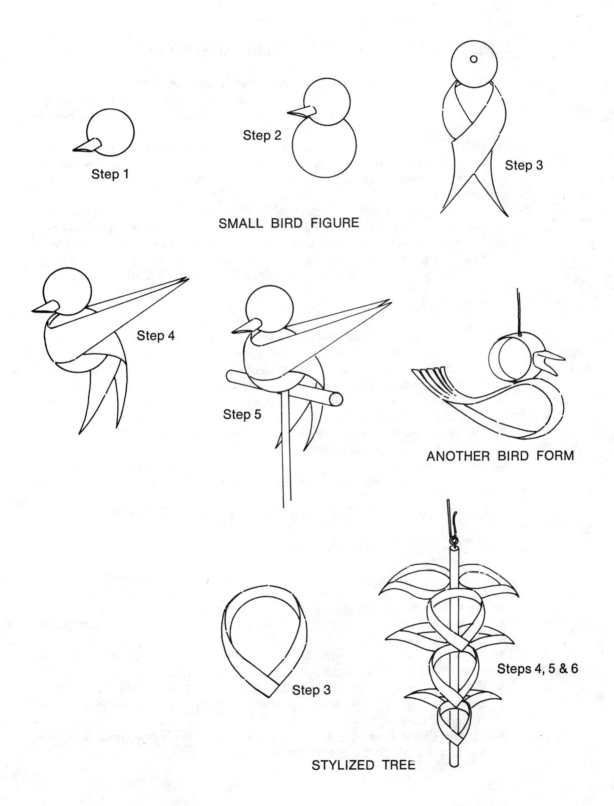

Step 1

Step 2

Step 3

SMALL BIRD FIGURE

Step 4

Step 5

ANOTHER BIRD FORM

Step 3

Steps 4, 5 & 6

STYLIZED TREE

SPLIT-STRAW MOSAICS AND APPLIQUE

In Poland, Indonesia, India, Greece, and other countries, flattened split straws are commonly used for decorating greeting cards, wall plaques, etc. These designs range from the very simple to the very complex and from the highly stylized to the realistic.

A Polish immigrant, The Reverend Marian Paskowicz of Reading, Pennsylvania, does very intricate, realistic "straw paintings" using oat, rye, wheat, millet, and barley straw to provide a range of shades and textures for his compositions.

In the Spanish Southwest, gold inlay, or marquetry, was commonly used to embellish chests and other pieces of furniture. In areas where gold was not available, straw was used effectively as a substitute. Examples of furniture decorated with straw may be seen in the museums of the Southwest today.

Split-straw appliqué may be done either on mounted fabric or on wood.

—DESIGNING ON FABRIC

1 Mount dark-colored fabric by stretching it over cardboard. Cut the fabric to extend ½ inch beyond the cardboard. Miter the corners of the fabric. Spread glue on the back ½-inch margin of the cardboard. Fold the ½-inch extension of the fabric to the back and glue it down.
2 Using a razor blade, X-Acto knife, paper punch, or nail clippers, cut shapes from flattened split straws.
3 Lay on a design, trying various arrangements. (Pay attention to the direction of the ridges in the straw.)
4 When you are satisfied with your composition, pick up and glue down one piece at a time without disturbing the rest of the design. (Use tweezers to help handle small pieces.)
5 Weight the finished piece down and allow it to dry overnight.

—DESIGNING ON WOOD

Pineapple Pattern

1 Back ¼-inch strips of split straw with masking tape.
2 Form small rhombus shapes by making slanted cuts ¼ inch apart across the strips of straw.
3 Arrange these in the shape of stylized pineapples. (Take special care to have all ridges in the straw running in the same direction.)
4 Cut simple leaf shapes and position them at the base and top of each pineapple. You may wish to repeat the pineapple unit to make a border design or all-over pattern.
5 Lay out the total design, then pick up and glue down one piece at a time without disturbing the other pieces.

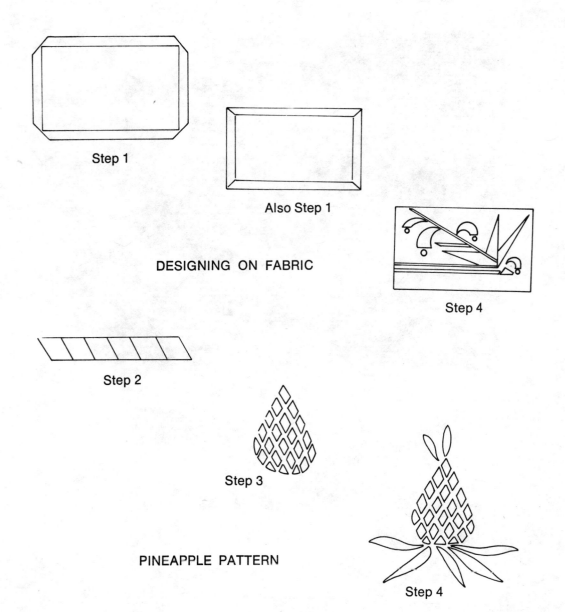

Step 1

Also Step 1

DESIGNING ON FABRIC

Step 4

Step 2

Step 3

PINEAPPLE PATTERN

Step 4

SPLIT-STRAW EARRINGS—STEP 5.

SPLIT-STRAW FIGURE ON FABRIC (FROM INDONESIA).

Wheat Pattern

1 Develop the wheat pattern by using ¼-inch rhombus shapes.
2 Cut very narrow strips along the ridges in the straw to make wheat beards and stems.
3 Add 2 long, pointed leaves, one on each side of a stem.
4 Carefully lay out the whole composition before gluing any part down. Dip 1 piece at a time into white glue and stick it down without disturbing the rest of the composition.

Grape Pattern

1 Back strips of split straw with masking tape.
2 Using paper punches, cut at least 2 sizes of circles. Save the negative shapes, the strips with the holes punched out, and use them as border decoration.
3 Arrange the circles to form clusters of grapes. Value contrasts can be achieved by placing the circles so that their ridges run in different directions.
4 Complete the grape clusters by topping them with a stem and 2 stylized grape leaves.
5 Without disturbing the total composition, pick up and glue down 1 piece at a time.

Old English Monograms

Old English letters are largely straight-line letters and can, therefore, be cut quite easily from flattened straws.

1 Back several strips of split straw (lying side by side) with a single strip of masking tape.
2 Using a paper pattern as a guide, cut out the desired letters from the prepared strips of straw.
3 Lay the cut letters on the surface they are to decorate. When a suitable arrangement is found, glue them down.
4 Use punched circles and very thin strips of straw to complete the composition.

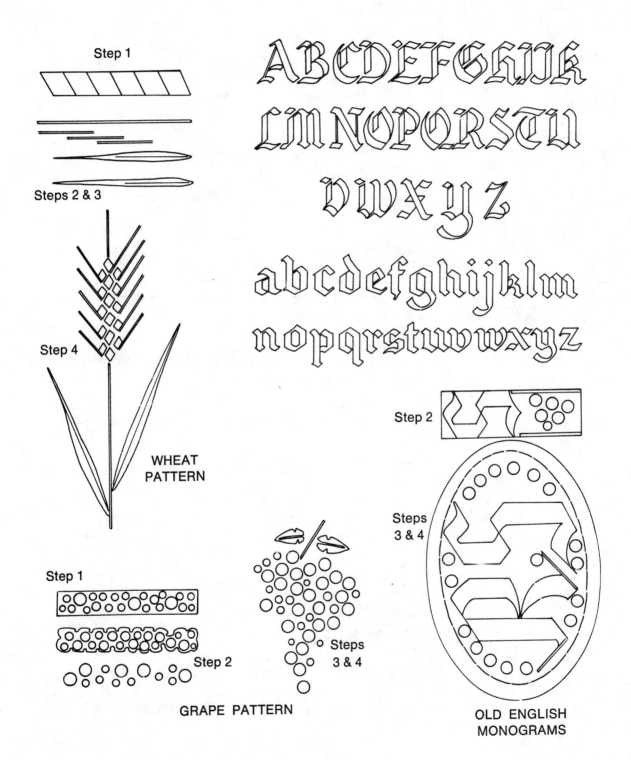

Step 1

Steps 2 & 3

Step 4

WHEAT
PATTERN

𝔄𝔅ℭ𝔇𝔈𝔉𝔊ℌℑ𝔎
𝔏𝔐𝔑𝔒𝔓𝔔𝔕𝔖𝔗𝔘
𝔙𝔚𝔛𝔜𝔷

abcdefghijklm
nopqrstuvwxyz

Step 2

Steps
3 & 4

Step 1

Step 2

Steps
3 & 4

GRAPE PATTERN

OLD ENGLISH
MONOGRAMS

Ornamented Wooden Box

1 Cut long, pointed ovals from a length of split straw that has been backed with masking tape to prevent splitting. Take great care not to damage the negative background shapes.
2 Arrange the ovals on the box and glue them down.
3 Use the negative background shapes as border patterns.
4 Decorate the lid with some of the same shapes. Make flower forms by cutting an oval across the middle. Set these between pairs of long oval leaves. Accent with punched circles and their negative shapes.

Oval Plaques

1 Cut isosceles triangles from a length of split straw backed with masking tape. There will be no waste except at the ends of the strip because the negative and positive shapes will be alike.
2 Arrange these triangles with their vertices pointed inward around the circumference of an oval-shaped wooden plaque a short distance in from its edge. (Watch the direction of the ridges.)
3 Glue one at a time into place without disturbing the others.
4 Decorate the center of the oval with other split-straw shapes, with straw sunbursts, sequins, or with any other harmonizing materials.

Mosaics

1 Cut triangles, rhombuses, circles, and other simple geometric shapes from reinforced split straws.
2 Combine these shapes into elaborate mosaiclike decorations for wooden trays, wooden plates, wooden spoon handles, picture frames, or small chests.
3 Use protective sheets of glass or coats of lacquer over the straw work on trays or other pieces that will be handled frequently. Wooden boxes decorated with straw and used for purses should have 20 coats of lacquer such as Cote and Tote® by Cunningham Art Products of Atlanta, Georgia.

Straw Pictures

The same gluing-on process as was used with flattened straw may be used successfully with scraps of round straws. The result resembles yarn stitchery.

1 Lay out odd scraps of straw saved from previous work.
2 Place the lengths side by side on a dark background in experimental arrangements of stylized plant and animal forms.
3 Lay on very short circular cross sections of straw for eyes, flower petals, and other accents.
4 Dip 1 piece at a time into glue and stick it down without disturbing the other pieces in the composition.

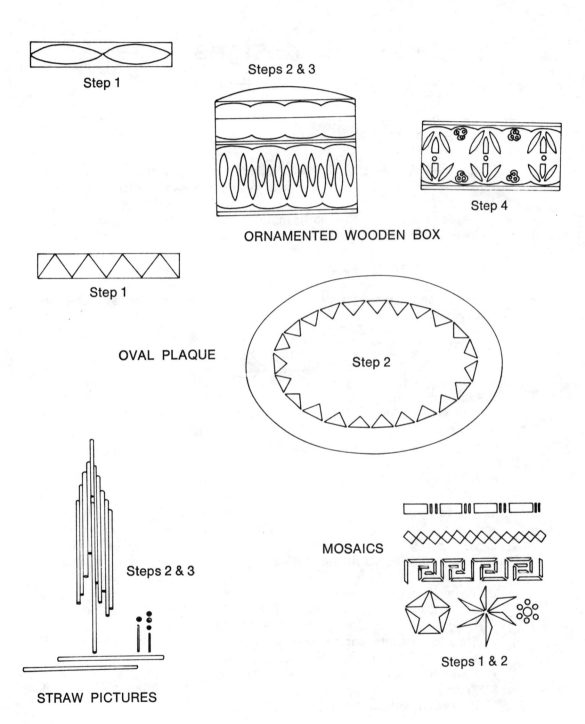

Step 1

Steps 2 & 3

Step 4

ORNAMENTED WOODEN BOX

Step 1

OVAL PLAQUE

Step 2

MOSAICS

Steps 2 & 3

Steps 1 & 2

STRAW PICTURES

braided-straw designs

BRAIDED-STRAW ORNAMENTS

1 Review braiding instructions under Basic Techniques.
2 Select soaked straws of equal thicknesses. Make a 5-straw braid 20 inches long.
3 Cut the strip into 5 4-inch lengths and fold each in the center.
4 Arrange these 5 folded strips (with cut ends toward the center) in a star pattern.
5 Staple or sew each cut end to that of an adjacent folded strip.
6 Wire a straw sunburst or other suitable ornament to the center when all the strips are joined.
7 Attach a cord for hanging.

The illustrations suggest other straw ornaments that can be assembled from strips of 5-straw braid.

STRAW ANGELS

Straw angels similar to the one in the drawing are made by Tarascan Indians at Tzin Tzin Tzan, a village on the shores of Lake Patzcura, about 150 miles west of Mexico City. Braided straw is used in both the head and the base of this figure. Tying and weaving techniques (see Basic Techniques) are used in making the rest of the figure.

HARVEST KNOT

The harvest knot is a ceremonial ornament traditionally worn by both men and women at harvest time in Ireland. The grain head is incorporated into the harvest knot worn by the woman but is absent in the ones worn by the men. You will appreciate its rhythmic lines in addition to its symbolic significance.

1 To begin, review Braiding under Basic Techniques.
2 Select soaked straws of equal thicknesses. Make a 20-inch length of 5-straw braid and a 12-inch length of 3-straw braid.
3 Tie a loose knot using the strip of 5-straw braid (see the illustration). Tie the same kind of knot from the strip of 3-straw braid.
4 Fasten the small knot in front of the large one.
5 Tie grain heads to the bottom of the ornament to intermingle with the unbraided ends of the strips.

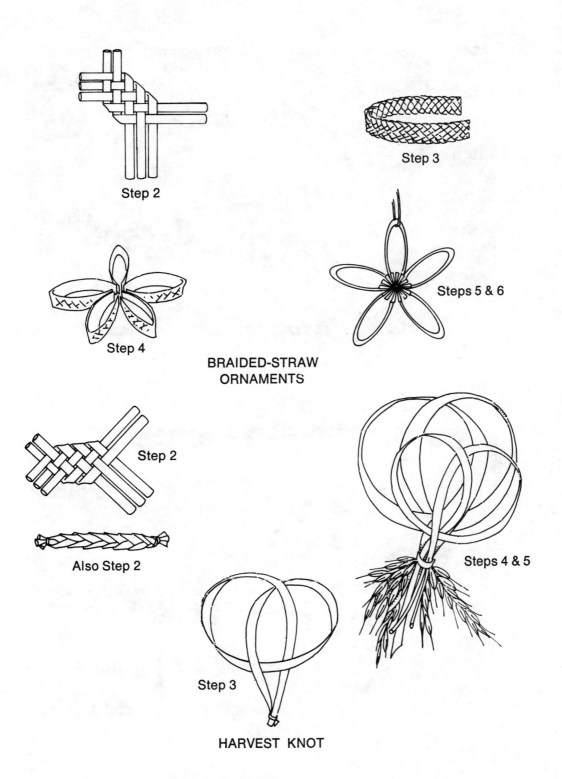

Step 2

Step 3

Step 4

Steps 5 & 6

**BRAIDED-STRAW
ORNAMENTS**

Step 2

Also Step 2

Steps 4 & 5

Step 3

HARVEST KNOT

BRAIDED STRAW.

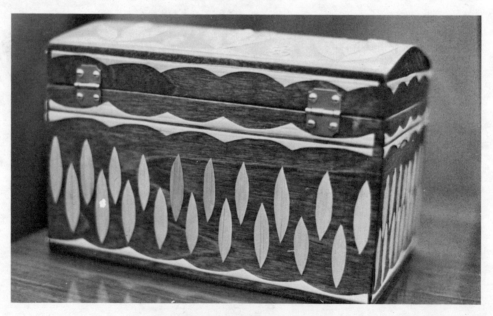

ORNAMENTED WOODEN BOX.

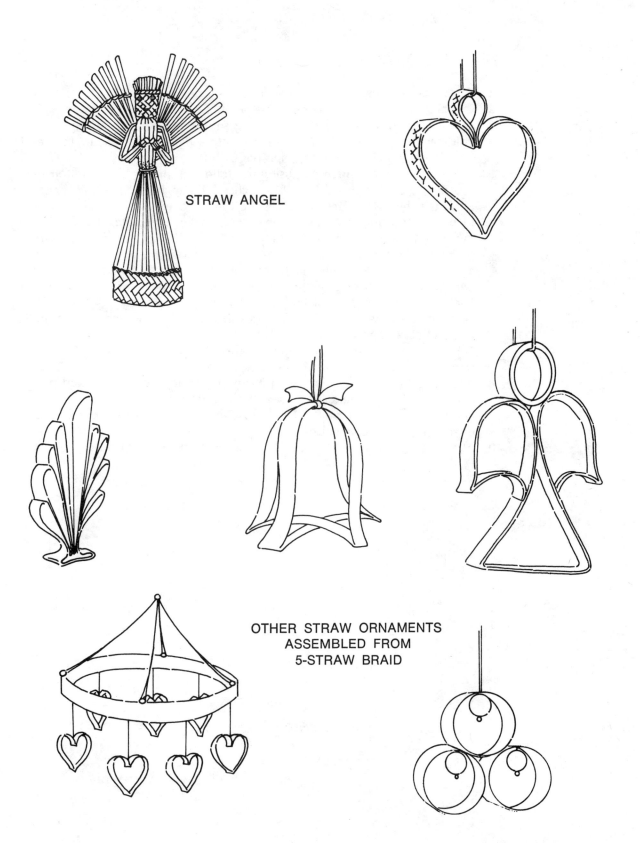

STRAW ANGEL

OTHER STRAW ORNAMENTS
ASSEMBLED FROM
5-STRAW BRAID

THE HANDBAG

1 Select soaked straws of equal thicknesses.
2 Prepare a total of 1754 inches of 3-straw braid.
3 Cut 58 strips of the braid 25 inches long and 38 strips 8 inches long.
4 Fold each strip in its middle and roll it into a tight spiral rosette and secure it with a pin or small wooden peg.
5 Prepare a canvas or linen bag using the following proportions: bottom—3½ inches by 9 inches; side—8½ inches by 9 inches; end—3½ inches by 8½ inches. Reinforce the sides, bottom, and ends (to a height of 4 inches) with stiffening under the lining. Make 2 handles (each 13½ inches long when finished) by threading 2 19-inch lengths of heavy wire through the wooden beads and leaving a loop of wire at each end. Run a paper fastener through the lining and stiffening and on through the wire loop in each end of the handles. Bend the ends of the fasteners back to secure the ends of the handles in place.
6 Arrange 25 of the larger straw rosettes in rows of 5 on each side of the bag and glue or sew them into place.
7 Fill in the spaces left by the larger rosettes with the smaller ones. Glue or sew them into place.
8 Arrange 4 of the larger rosettes in 2 rows of 2 each on the stiffened part of the ends of the bag. Glue or sew these into place.
9 Fill in the spaces left by the larger rosettes with the smaller ones. Glue or sew them into place also.
10 Attach a covered button-and-loop fastener at the top to complete the bag.

Step 2

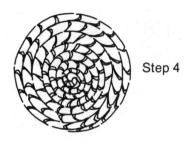

Step 4

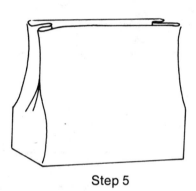

Step 5

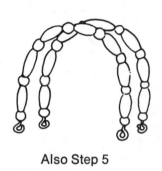

Also Step 5

THE HANDBAG

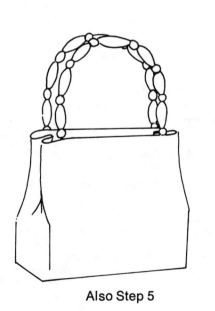

Also Step 5

Steps 6, 7, 8 & 9

STRAW MAT

The finished mat will be a circle 9½ inches in diameter.

1 Prepare 208 inches of 5-straw braid for the outside loops of the border and 125 inches of the same for the inside loops.
2 Make 83 scallops 1¼ inches deep from the 208-inch strip and 83 scallops ¾ inch deep from the 125-inch strip.
3 Mesh the short scallops into the longer ones and thread a heavy cord through the length of accordioned braids. Tie the ends of the cord to form a 9½-inch diameter circle with the small scallops inside.
4 Fill the open center with rosettes, scallops, or other shapes made from 5-straw braid strips. Stitch these all together or glue them to a felt backing.

STRAW HAT NO. 1

1 Select a sizable quantity of soaked straws of equal thicknesses. (These should be long, thick straws.)
2 Prepare a 120-inch strip of 7-straw braid. (See instructions under Braiding —Basic Techniques.)
3 Arrange the finished braid into a loose, flat, spiral shape.
4 Push the loops together at one point and allow them to spread apart elsewhere. There should be 6 loops of different sizes.
5 Stitch the loops together at the point where they touch, or slip them up (telescope-fashion) and stitch them in a slightly overlapping position. This becomes the back of the hat.
6 String straw beads, wooden beads, or fabric-covered styrofoam balls between loops to hold them apart.
7 Decorate the back with ribbon, net, or other suitable materials.

Pioneer mothers commonly made by hand all straw hats for their families to wear both for everyday and for dress occasions. At harvest time a headed sheaf of grain straw was brought into the house where the straws were husked and soaked. Then the straws were made into long braids that were finally coiled and stitched to fit the heads of family members. Some families had wooden straw-flattening machines that the children could operate to facilitate the preparation of the straw for the braiding. Examples of these interesting pieces of equipment can be seen in museums of Pennsylvania and New York State today.

The following instructions will enable you to create a custom-made straw hat for yourself or for a friend.

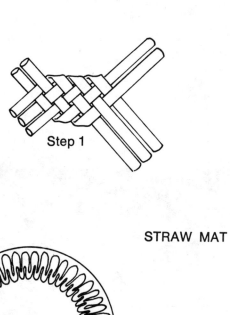

Step 1

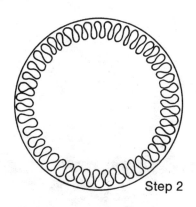

Step 2

STRAW MAT

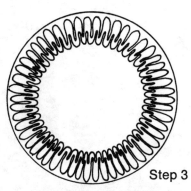

Step 3

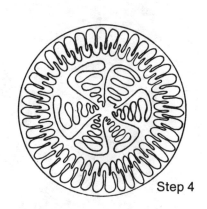

Step 4

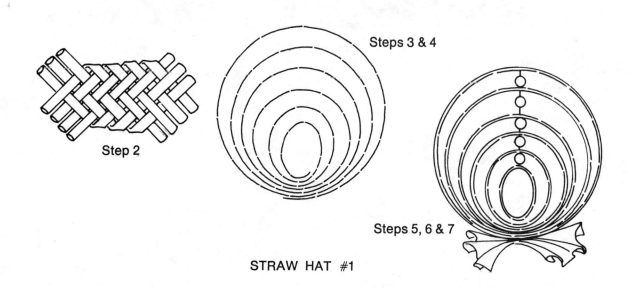

Step 2

Steps 3 & 4

Steps 5, 6 & 7

STRAW HAT #1

STRAW MAT—STEP 4.

THE HANDBAG.

STRAW HAT NO. 2

1 Select the thickest and longest straws you have and soak them well.

2 Prepare 288 inches of 9-straw braid; the braid should be about 1¼ inches wide. Follow step-by-step instructions for making 9-straw braids (see Basic Techniques). Be sure to splice at well-spaced intervals to prevent weak spots from occurring in the braid. Hold the braid flat on a firm surface, especially while splicing. Be generous with splicing straws; extraneous ends can be cut off after the hat is finished.

3 Begin constructing the hat at the center of the crown. If the braid has dried, soak it again for 30 minutes before proceeding. Using a long darning needle and doubled twine string, insert a drawstring between the layers of wet straw at one edge of the braid. Pass this drawstring through 6 inches of the braid at first; then keep advancing it as the work progresses.

4 Pull the drawstring firmly and steadily until that edge of the braid is crowded into a circle about the size of a dime. Press the circle of braid with a warm iron until it is fairly dry.

5 Working on the inside of the crown, stitch the beginning end of the braid down and continue spiraling the braid outward, threading more drawstring into the edge as you go. (As this string is used up, tie on another piece with a firm, small knot and continue.)

6 Use a curved upholstery needle threaded with ecru crochet cotton or twine string for attaching the strips of braid together as they spiral around. (A straight needle will not dig into the flat surfaces and come out easily.)

7 Continue to work on the inside of the crown. Attach the spiraling braid to each previous round, using a catch stitch. The outside edge of the braid should overhang the spiral slightly on the outside surface of the crown.

8 Pull the drawstring, and press regularly as the work progresses. This will keep the crown flat on top.

9 After the braid has gone around 3 times, begin to let the crown pull in to fit the head. Accomplish this by pulling less on the drawstring.

10 Cut a temporary brim from corrugated cardboard. Make the hole fit the head comfortably.

11 After the braid has circled 5 or 6 times, put a second drawstring into the bottom edge of the crown and pull the braid up to fit the head hole in the temporary cardboard brim.

12 Press the gathered edge until it is nearly dry. Fasten that drawstring with a few stitches and a knot; then clip it off. (The cardboard brim is no longer needed.)

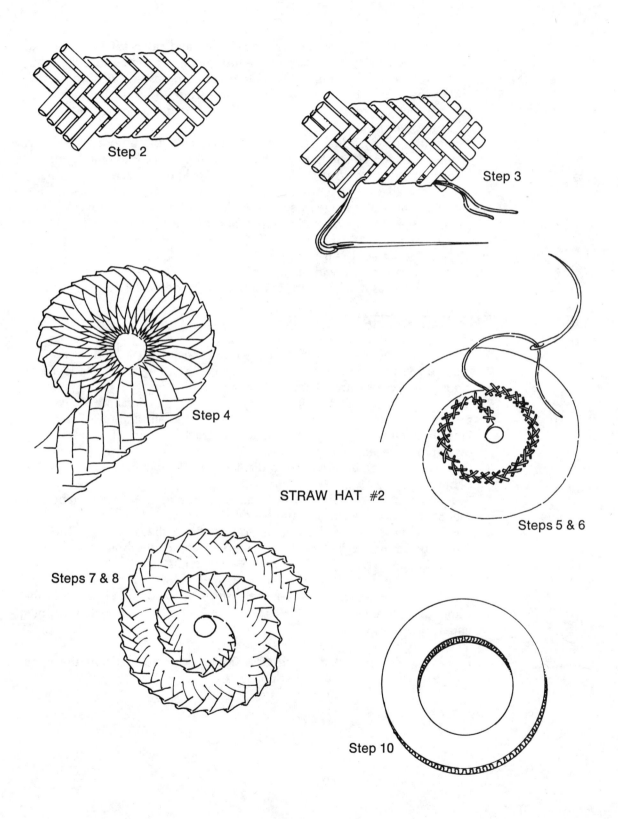

Step 2

Step 3

Step 4

STRAW HAT #2

Steps 5 & 6

Steps 7 & 8

Step 10

13 Without cutting the braid, continue spiraling and catch-stitching to make the brim. Keep the drawstring at the inside edge of the braid pulled taut enough to make the brim lie flat as the work progresses. Press frequently. Make the brim 4 braid widths wide in the front and 3 in the back. (The proportions are more interesting if the front of the brim is made wider than the back.)

14 Spiral the braid gradually to a termination under the brim as the end is approached. Catch-stitch across the end of the braid. Press the brim.

15 From thin, wet straws, make a 5-straw braid long enough to go around the outer edge of the brim. Stitch this braid to the under side of the brim at the outer edge. Use ecru-colored thread and a thin needle. Stitches will not show on the upper side of the brim if they follow the line of the straws.

16 Prepare a 5-straw braid from thin straws for a hatband.

17 Catch-stitch a 1-inch-wide length of grosgrain ribbon to the inside edge of the crown as a sweatband. Experiment with other designs for hats.

BRAIDED-STRAW BASKET

1 Select a large quantity of straws of equal thicknesses. Soak them well.

2 Prepare 256 inches of 5-straw braid. (Review Braiding under Basic Techniques.) Make an extra 44 inches for the handle.

3 Soak the braid well so that it can be shaped without breaking straws. Beginning at the center of the base, catch-stitch the strips into a flat spiral. Press frequently to flatten the braids. Let each section of braid slightly overlap the preceding layer as it spirals.

4 Continue until the base reaches a diameter of 3½ inches (about 4 rounds of braid).

5 Begin to spiral the braid upward and continue for 2¾ inches (about 6 rounds) to make the sides of the basket.

6 Fan the braids out for the rim as you continue the stitching. (The rim should be about 2½ inches wide.) Taper the end of the braid out of sight under the rim. Press the rim flat or into a rippled pattern.

7 For the handle, cut the 44-inch strip of braid into 2 22-inch lengths. Lay a 22-inch length of wire between the 2 strips of braid and stitch them together at their edges. Bend this handle into a neat arc and fasten its ends under the rim of the basket.

Flower-pot covers and drinking-glass holders can be made in the same way if the rim and handle are omitted.

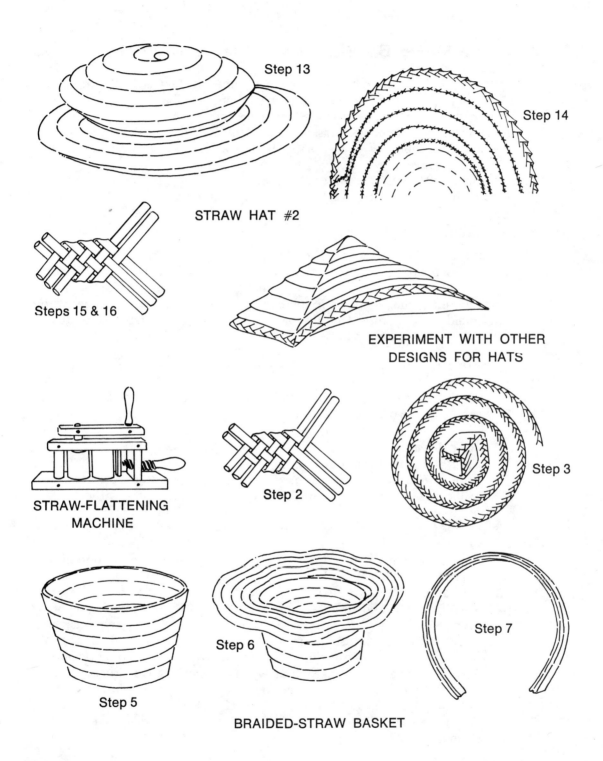

Step 13

Step 14

STRAW HAT #2

Steps 15 & 16

EXPERIMENT WITH OTHER
DESIGNS FOR HATS

STRAW-FLATTENING
MACHINE

Step 2

Step 3

Step 5

Step 6

Step 7

BRAIDED-STRAW BASKET

BAGS MADE BY WEAVING WITH STRAW BRAID

Straw braids were spiraled and stitched together at their edges in the construction of the basket and the hat. In making the handbag with the wooden-bead handles, the braids were rolled into coils and attached to a fabric foundation. A third and somewhat easier method for utilizing the straw braid is in weaving. The choice of width for the braid will depend on the scale of the piece being woven.

Simple flat mats may be woven from straw braids and the edges bound with fabric or with strips of finer braid than is used in the body of the mat.

—HANDBAG

An attractive handbag may be made by shaping and assembling 3 mats woven from straw braids. One large mat (about 18 inches by 23 inches) makes the body of the bag and 2 small mats (5½ inches by 6½ inches) make the ends. Stitch these together as shown in the illustration. Cover unfinished edges with finer braided-straw strips. Line the bag with a harmonizing fabric and attach a strip of webbing for a handle.

—SHOULDER BAG

A shoulder bag may be made without seams by beginning at the bottom and weaving it into the desired shape.

1 Review instructions under Basic Techniques for 7-straw braid.
2 Using straw of medium thickness, prepare 6 26-inch strips and 8 30-inch strips of 7-straw braid for the base and vertical supports. Prepare another 580 inches in one continuous braid for use in weaving the vertical sides of the bag. Each braid will be about ½ inch in width.
3 Lay the 8 strips side by side in one direction and the 6 strips at right angles to them.
4 Weave the center part of these strips together to form the flat bottom of the bag.
5 This leaves 28 ends to provide vertical supports for the sides of the bag.
6 Since there must be an odd number of supports for the weaving to proceed properly, begin by laying a 10-inch tail of the 580-inch braid parallel to one of the 8 supports. This makes a total of 29 verticals. Set all these at right angles to the base as the weaving progresses. There should be about ¾ inch between the vertical strips when the weaving is finished.
7 Proceed to weave around and around with the remaining 570-inch strip to build up the sides of the bag.
8 When the braid is used up, tuck the end under an adjacent edge and stitch it into place.

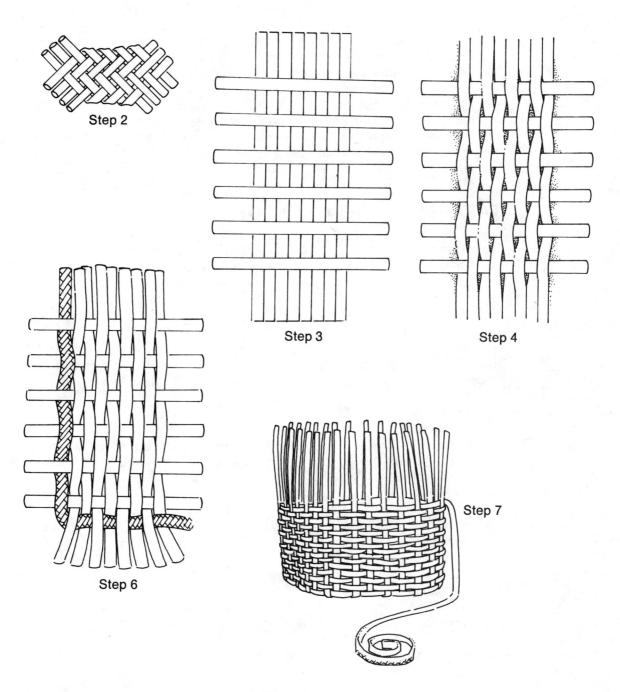

Step 2

Step 3

Step 4

Step 6

Step 7

SHOULDER BAG

9 About an inch of each support should be standing above the last round of braid. Fold each end inside and stitch it down.
10 Prepare an additional 30 inches of the braid and stitch it over the 29 ends that were folded inside.
11 Cut a suitable lining and shape it to fit the bag. Stitch it to the top of the bag just beneath the finishing braid. The finished bag will measure about 9 inches in height and the base will be about 6 inches by 11 inches.
12 One hundred and eight inches of 1¼-inch webbing will make 2 shoulder straps.

plaited-straw spirals

Somewhat related to the technique of braiding is the technique of plaiting straw spirals. Examples of the use of these spirals in decorations for harvest festivals can be found in Egypt, England, and elsewhere.

EGYPTIAN FERTILITY SYMBOL

As soon as the wheat has headed out and while it is still green, Egyptian children go to the fields and cut off the head sections of the plants at the first nodes. From these they fashion fresh fertility symbols to hang in the house to replace the ones that had been hanging since the previous spring. The design is suggestive of a human figure.

1 To make this straw symbol, select 30 terminal straws, each about 15 inches in length, with the heads attached. Remove the husks and set the stems in a jar of water to soak.
2 Begin by laying 2 straws together with heads at opposite ends from each other.
3 Tie a straw or cord in the middle to hold the straws together and to be used later for hanging.
4 Five and one-half inches from its head, make a sharp bend in a straw and fold it over the 2 tied straws very close to the cord and on the right side of it.
5 Bend the straw again and fold it sharply to the left beneath the 2 tied straws, cross it over itself, and leave it lying parallel to the tied straws and close beneath them.
6 Turn the whole structure over and work on the back of it.

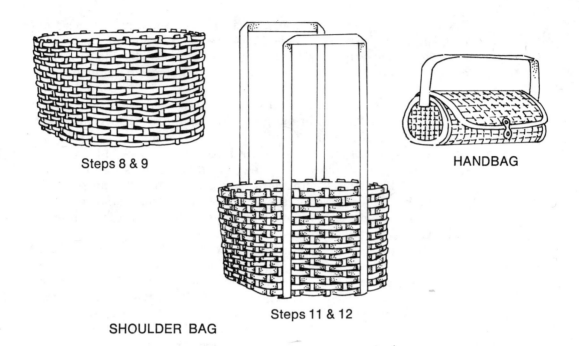

Steps 8 & 9

HANDBAG

SHOULDER BAG

Steps 11 & 12

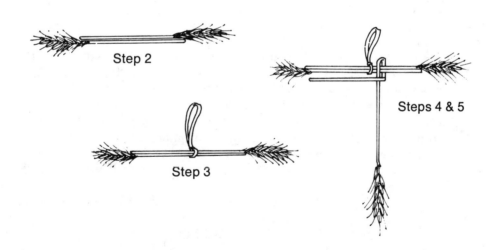

Step 2

Step 3

Steps 4 & 5

EGYPTIAN FERTILITY SYMBOL

7 Pick another headed straw from the jar. Five and one-half inches from the grain head, make a sharp bend in this second straw and loop it over the 2 tied straws very close to the cord and on the right side of it. (The first straw used is now at the left of the cord since the structure was turned over.)

8 Bend the second straw again and fold it sharply to the left beneath the 2 tied straws and the end of the first straw bent. Cross it over itself and leave it lying parallel to the 3.

9 Again, turn the whole structure over and work on the back of it.

10 Pick a third straw from the jar. Proceed exactly as in steps 7 and 8.

11 Continue picking straws from the jar and adding them to the structure, following instructions given in steps 7 and 8. (Each time a straw is added, it locks the preceding straw into place and adds both width and length to the plaited portion of the figure.)

12 When all 30 straws have been used, secure the end of the last straw and cut off uneven ends on the right and left sides of the structure. If some straws are too short, telescope others in to lengthen them. The plaited area measures about 4½ inches across and 2½ inches deep. The total figure measures about 8½ inches across and 10½ inches deep. The line of grain heads at the bottom of the structure is more interesting if it forms a shallow V-shape rather than a straight line.

CORN DOLLIES

The making of plaited straw spirals (see Basic Techniques) as a folk craft dates back to antiquity in European countries. An interesting example is the "corn dolly," which is still used as a decorative symbol in both the churches and the homes of England during the harvest celebrations.

Traditionally, each grain field was thought to contain a "Spirit of Fertility" that would die when the last sheaf was cut unless it was housed in a "corn dolly" (made from the last bundle of grain cut) and kept until the next harvest. It was customarily made by the oldest harvester and hung in the kitchen of the home. At the time of the next harvest it was fed to the best cow or mare.

A variation of the "corn dolly" was the "harvest maiden." Elizabeth Goudge in her book, *Gentian Hill,* a story of life in Southwestern England at the time of the French Revolution, tells of the harvest, which ended with the placing of the "harvest maiden" on the last sheaf:

The reapers were busy in the wheat field to the right of Bowery Hill. . . .
The reaping hook, larger and broader than the common sickle, was held
in the mower's right hand and his left arm gathered the standing corn.

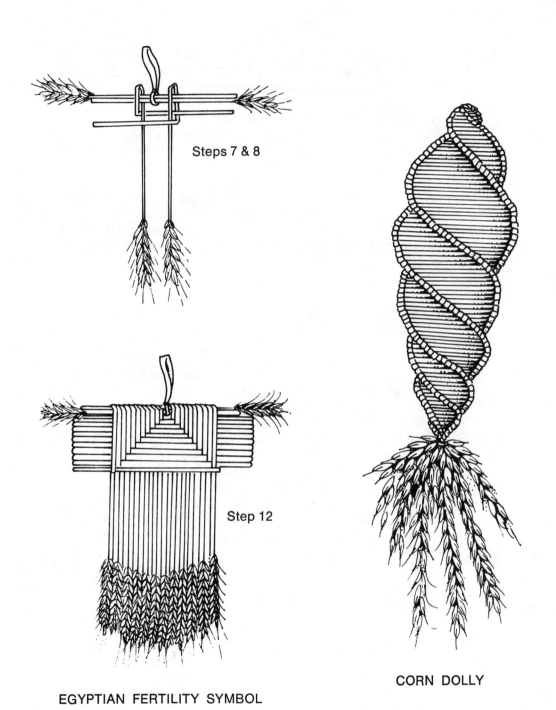

Steps 7 & 8

Step 12

EGYPTIAN FERTILITY SYMBOL

CORN DOLLY

The sweep of the hook, the encircling movement of the left arm, the bend and rise of the body, had the rhythm of music, and the curve of the golden hill against the blue sky was part of it.

. . . . . .

It was from their Roman conquerors that the British had learned how to collect their sheaves of corn in stacks in the field that it might dry and harden before it was housed, with the heads turned inwards in the form of a pyramid to shed the rain.

. . . . . .

The farms of the district did their reaping by turns, all of them helping each other. . . . By five o'clock the cutting of the wheat was over, and they all sat in the shade of the trees and ate the special harvest cakes that Mother Spriggs had baked for them, washed down with yet more liquid refreshment, and then the binding of the sheaves went on until the evening.

. . . . . .

"They're finished," Stella cried. "Look, Sol! Father Spriggs is making the Maiden."

. . . . . .

Father Spriggs had bound up a sheaf in rough imitation of the human form and set it upon the central stack. This was the harvest goddess, Demeter, though none of the reapers knew that. The doctor, had he been present, would have quoted Theocritus: "Ah, once again may I plant the great fan on the corn heap, while she stands smiling by, Demeter of the threshing floor, with sheaves and poppies in her hands." When the maiden was in place, the reapers flung their sickles up in the air towards her, and the sun, glinting on them, made them look like half-moons falling about her. "We ha' in! We ha' in!" they yelled, and the triumphant shout echoed over the hills to tell the countryside that yet another farmer's corn was safely stacked. Then, cheering and singing, they tramped towards the farmhouse, where they would eat and drink and enjoy themselves until one o'clock in the morning.[1]

[1] From *Gentian Hill* by Elizabeth Goudge, by permission of the publishers, Coward McCann & Geoghegan, Inc., 200 Madison Avenue, N.Y. Copyright 1949.

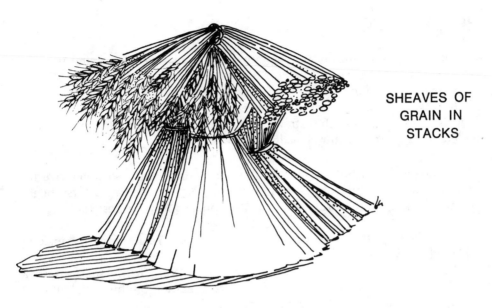

SHEAVES OF
GRAIN IN
STACKS

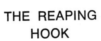

THE REAPING
HOOK

THE STYLIZED TREE

The stylized tree sculpture is an adaptation of the plaited-straw spiral used in the figure of the "corn dolly." Review Plaiting Straw Spirals under Basic Techniques before beginning this piece. Thick straws are suitable for large trees and thin ones for small ones. However, a more rhythmic effect can be achieved by grading from thin straws at the top through thicker straws at the middle and back to thin straws at the base.

The beginning of this structure is the only tedious part; so don't give up if your first attempt is frustrating. If thin straws seem too delicate at first, begin with larger ones. Sturdy forefinger- and thumbnails are your best tools.

1 Follow step-by-step the instructions under Basic Techniques for making plaited-straw spirals.
2 When only a small opening remains at the bottom of the spiral, push a ¼-inch wooden dowel through the hollow center of the spiral until it touches the opposite end, where the spiral began.
3 Continue the plaiting of the straws until the squares are tight against the dowel. Then fold the four ends down against the dowel and tie them securely in place before you clip off the extra straw. The fifth straw is locked into place by one of the 4 straws. Cut the dowel off so that the exposed trunk of the tree is about half the height of the spiral.
4 Find a circle of wood for a base. (See Suppliers.) Sand it smooth. Drill a hole in the center large enough to receive the ¼-inch dowel. Glue the dowel into place.

Groupings of these tree forms in several sizes make an attractive center of interest in a room.

SPIRAL DROP EARRINGS

1 Select 5 very thin, long straws of equal thicknesses. (The use of very long straws will eliminate the need for splicing.) Soak them well.
2 Plait them into neat spirals, following the step-by-step instructions under Basic Techniques.
3 Complete several of these small, plaited spirals, making each about 2 inches long. Select the 2 that match best and use them for the pair of earrings.
4 Fit gold-colored bell caps (see Suppliers) over the tied ends of these spirals and wire the caps to the eyelets of drop earclips.

These earrings are very pleasant to wear because of their light weight.

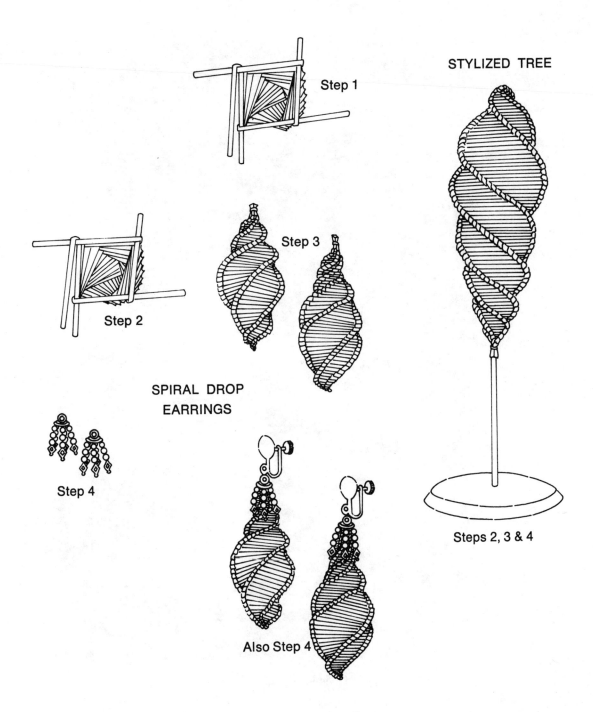

Step 1

STYLIZED TREE

Step 3

Step 2

SPIRAL DROP
EARRINGS

Step 4

Also Step 4

Steps 2, 3 & 4

SPIRAL DROP EARRINGS.

STYLIZED TREES.

SPIRAL WREATH

1   Tie together at their tips 5 straws of equal thicknesses.
2   Begin plaiting them into a spiral, following instructions under Basic Techniques.
3   Gradually increase the width until it reaches the thickness of a broom handle.
4   Then fit this piece over the tip of the broom handle and continue building the plaited spiral around the handle of the broom. The broom handle serves as a guide to keep a uniform thickness throughout the length of the spiral.
5   Continue plaiting until the desired length (about 30 inches) is reached.
6   Carefully push (don't pull) the finished piece off the broom handle.
7   Wrap the length of plaited spiral around a can or jar (about 10 inches in diameter), and fasten its ends together to hold the wreath in a circular shape until it dries.
8   Decorate the wreath with harmonizing ribbons or plant materials.

MORNING GLORIES

During the making of plaited-straw spirals, be sure to look inside the figure as it progresses. The inside is as intriguing as the outside. Partly finished pieces suggest bells or morning glory blossoms.

1   To make this straw flower, begin by tying 7 soaked straws of equal thicknesses together near their tips.
2   Plait these straws into a spiral following instructions under Basic Techniques.
3   After the plaiting has progressed a short distance, begin to widen rapidly to give a dramatic flair to the lip of the blossom. (See instructions for widening under Plaiting Straw Spirals—Basic Techniques.)
4   Notice the lacy effect created by wide spacing of straws. Accomplish this by moving out a short distance on a straw before making the sharp bend in it.
5   Tie the last straw used to an adjacent straw. Clip the free end-straws to 1-inch lengths.
6   Finally, attach a stem wire to the base of the blossom and cover this wire with narrow masking tape.

These straw morning glories, as well as closed straw spirals attached to stem wires, add intriguing accents to arrangements of dried plants such as wood roses, cornhusk flowers, and magnolia leaves.

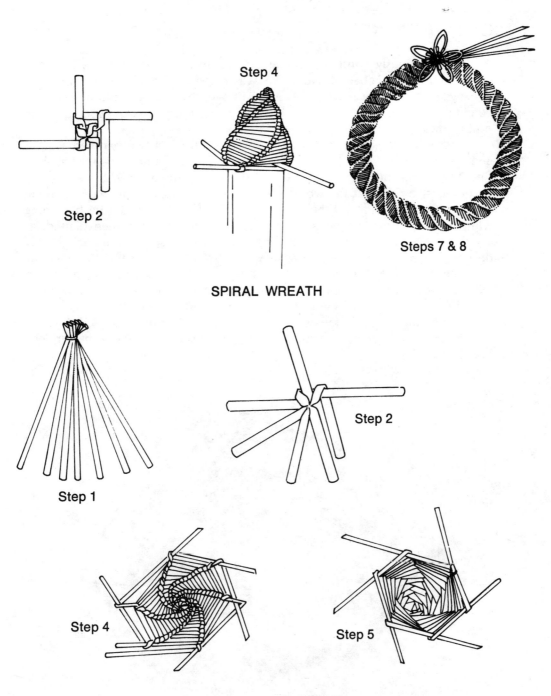

Step 4

Step 2

Steps 7 & 8

SPIRAL WREATH

Step 1

Step 2

Step 4

Step 5

MORNING GLORY

STRAW BASKET

A most ingeniously contrived basket created from oat straw grown on her father's farm near Lebanon, Nebraska, was made by Mary Bradbury in 1885, a few years before her marriage. Despite its age, the basket is still in excellent condition. It is now a treasured possession of Mary's niece, Lois Carr, of Ames, Iowa.

The basket is hexagonal in shape and has a lid and two handles. The lid and bottom were made alike. Seven soaked straws were tied together at their tips. They were then plaited as explained under Plaiting Straw Spirals—Basic Techniques, except that the work was held flat and was not allowed to spiral.

The 6 vertical sides of the basket are alike. Each was made by beginning with 5 straws tied together at their tips. These straws were then plaited, as for the top and bottom, not allowing the work to spiral. The delightfully decorative handles and border spirals were also made using the plaited-straw spiral technique. However, this time the work was allowed to spiral and was held to a uniform width throughout, possibly with the aid of a wooden dowel or broom handle (see instructions for the spiral wreath).

Finally, the parts of the basket were carefully and firmly stitched together and the lid was hinged with a straw braid. The finished basket is a masterpiece of craftsmanship.

THE FINISHED BASKET OF OAK STRAW (NEBRASKA, 1885).

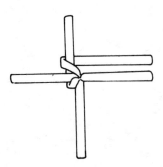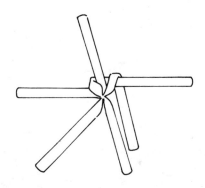

... BEGINNING WITH 5 STRAWS   SEVEN SOAKED STRAWS WERE TIED

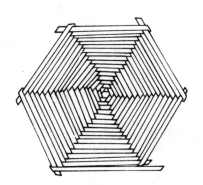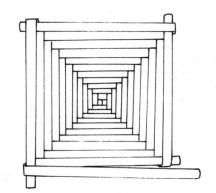

THEY WERE THEN PLAITED ...   THESE STRAWS WERE THEN PLAITED

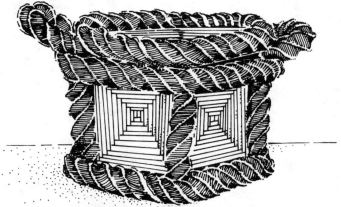

DECORATIVE HANDLES
& BORDER SPIRALS

THE FINISHED BASKET

now you are on your own

If this book has led you to see the natural beauty of straw and to sense its potential as a valid medium for creative artistry, you are ready to launch into a leisure-time activity that will give you hours of pleasure and a special niche among your craft-minded friends. Take a trip into the country and find a field of ripened grain or plant your own. Then set to work husking it and getting it sorted for the projects you are anticipating. Collect the few other materials listed in the front of this book and begin your new hobby. Refer frequently to the section, Basic Techniques, and see what you can invent with those few guides. You may come up with yet another chapter for this book.

the author

Ruth Straight Hibbs was born on March 12, 1918, in Portland, Oregon, but moved with her family in 1920 to a farm near Yarrow, Missouri. She and her sister and three brothers helped with the farm work during the summer months and attended a rural school the rest of the year. Her interest in working with natural materials developed as a result of this close association with plants and animals on the family farm.

After graduation from the Yarrow School, she and her sister walked daily to and from high school six miles from their farm home. During those long hours on the road, they observed the natural beauty of roadside grasses and flowers. Later, when they were art students, they recalled and incorporated into their creative expressions the lovely offerings of nature.

Ruth and her husband, Thom, head of the biology department at Georgia Southern College, and their five children now own the farmstead adjoining Ruth's childhood farm home and return there each summer to vacation. During those summer months, Ruth does numerous watercolor paintings and harvests her year's supply of rye straw.

Her experience in teaching strawcraft has been with the Craft Division of Faculty Women's Club at Iowa State University and at Georgia Southern College. In addition, she has taught this craft to county home economists, garden clubs, and numerous other groups. In Ames, Iowa, she also conducted workshops at the Ames Society for the Arts Galleries and presented a series of television programs on "Designing with Straw."

Her straw work was part of a "Festive Design" exhibition at Cornell University in 1965 and later was shown at the Savannah Art Association in Savannah, Georgia.

After completing work for the degrees, Bachelor of Arts and Bachelor of Science, at the Northeast Missouri State Teachers College and for the degree, Master of Fine Arts, at the University of Colorado, she taught art at the Northeast Missouri State Teachers College, at the University of Colorado, and at Cornell University. She later taught classes in watercolor painting at the Ames Society for the Arts in Ames, Iowa.

Her paintings have been exihibited in the Nelson Art Gallery of Kansas City, Missouri, City Art Museum of St. Louis, Missouri, Rochester Art Gallery of Rochester, New York, Telfair Academy of Arts Gallery of Savannah, Georgia, and on campuses of four universities.

As an illustrator, she has done drawings for a textbook and for two doctoral dissertations.